I Wanted to Know All about God

by Virginia L. Kroll
illustrated by Debra Reid Jenkins

Eerdmans Books for Young Readers
Grand Rapids Michigan/Cambridge, U.K.

Published 1994 by
Eerdmans Books for Young Readers
an imprint of
Wm. B. Eerdmans Publishing Co.
255 Jefferson Ave. S.E., Grand Rapids, Michigan 49503
P.O. Box 163, Cambridge CB3 9PU U.K.

Paperback edition 1998

Printed in Singapore

00   7   6   5   4

Spring Arbor Edition

Library of Congress Cataloging-in-Publication Data

Kroll, Virginia L.
I wanted to know all about God / by Virginia L. Kroll;
illustrated by Debra Reid Jenkins.
p.   cm.
ISBN 0-8028-5078-2 (cloth: alk. paper)
ISBN 0-8028-5166-5 (paper: alk. paper)
1. God — Juvenile Literature.   [1. God.]   I. Jenkins,
Debra Reid, ill.   II. Title.
BT107.K767   1994
231 — dc20   93-37382
                                         CIP
                                         AC

I wanted to know all about God,
so I went out looking for him in signs of his creation.

I wondered what God does in the mornings.
Then I smelled the dew on the grass at dawn.

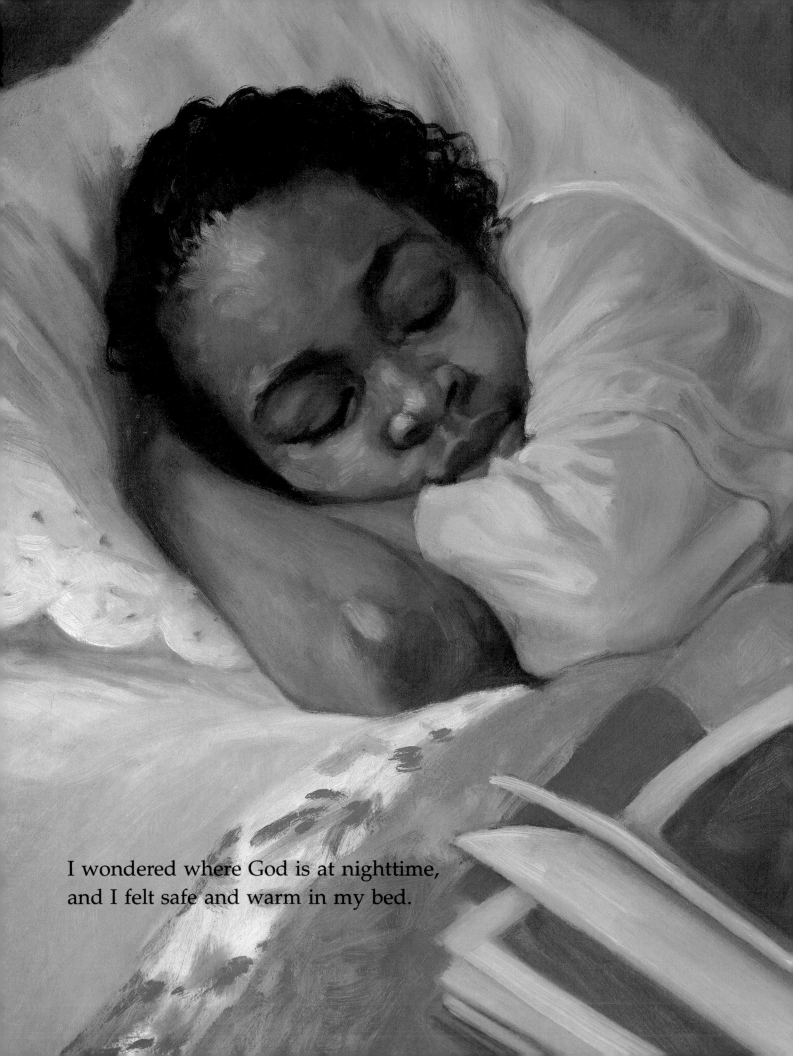

I wondered where God is at nighttime,
and I felt safe and warm in my bed.

I wondered if God is gentle,
and a butterfly floated on the air in front of me.

I wondered if God is strong,
and the ocean roared in my ears.

I wondered how God's reflection
looks when he smiles,
and the snow glittered in the sun.

I wanted to know if God likes music.
Then I heard a pond on a summer night.

I wondered if God likes art,
and I saw a spiderweb in my uncle's barn.

I wanted to know what colors God likes.
Then I met several children of other races.

I wondered how tall God makes his people,
and the girl next to me looked up and smiled.

I wondered if God's people have faith in each other, and my friend trusted me with a secret.

I wondered if God is caring,
and the new boy shared his crayons with me.

I wondered what God's love feels like,
and Grandma put her arms around me
and gave me a big hug.

I wanted to know where God likes to visit,
and I felt someone knocking at my heart.
Now when I go out looking for God,
I know exactly where to find him.

the best of Quilting Arts

Your Ultimate Resource for
Art Quilt Techniques and Inspiration

POKEY BOLTON

INTERWEAVE.
interweave.com

Editor	Elaine Lipson
Art Director	Liz Quan
Designer	Margaret McCullough
Photography	Larry Stein and Korday Studios (except where noted)
Production	Katherine Jackson

Front cover, top: Melody Johnson, *Leaf Light* (detail). Front cover, bottom: Frieda Anderson, *Dancing Trees* (detail). Back cover, top: Jane Dunnewold, *Breath* (detail). Back cover, bottom: Judy Coates Perez, *Untitled* (detail).

Interweave Press LLC
201 East Fourth Street
Loveland, CO 80537
interweave.com

Printed in China by C&C Offset

All of the articles in this collection were previously published in *Quilting Arts* magazine, © Interweave Press. Some have been altered to update information or conform to space limitations.

Except as otherwise noted, artwork is by the article's author.

Library of Congress Cataloging-in-Publication Data

Bolton, Patricia.
 The best of Quilting arts : your ultimate resource for art quilt techniques & inspiration / Pokey Bolton.
    p. cm.
 Includes bibliographical references and index.
 ISBN 978-1-59668-399-0 (pbk.)
 1. Quilting. 2. Art quilts--Design. I. Quilting arts. II. Title.
 TT835.B51435 2011
 746.46--dc23
                           2011021179

10 9 8 7 6 5 4 3 2 1

Acknowledgments

Quilting Arts magazine would not have come to be if it weren't for the passion and dedication of so many people who believed in this publication.

First and foremost, I'd like to extend my heartfelt thanks to my in-law family, the Boltons. Without all of their help and support over the years, *Quilting Arts* would never have gotten off its feet.

I would also like to thank my *Quilting Arts* family of co-workers and talented and giving artists who have contributed over the last ten years. What a fantastic, colorful, and fun journey. Here's to ten more!

Contents

Celebrate Ten Years of Quilting Arts

To knit or to quilt? That was the question I asked myself when I walked into a craft store ten years ago, looking for a much-needed break from my doctoral studies.

I perused the shelves of the store, walking briskly past the palettes of watercolor paints, bins of cake decorating tools, and aisle upon aisle of scrapbooking gadgetry, and I ultimately paused in the section that focused on fiber. As beckoning as those luscious piled skeins of yarns were, it was the colorful patterned bolts of fabric lined up like cheerful little soldiers along the wall that lured me. Quilting won over knitting, and during a holiday break from school, I converted my dining room into a temporary quilt studio and made my first quilt. As first efforts go, I realized I had quite a lot to learn. My machine stitching was wonky, my piecing was terribly uneven, my binding was pathetic, and my sense of color? We won't go there.

Having made this first quilt, though, I realized two things: I had a passion for textiles and a desire to create something unique with fabric and thread. That's when I started to research crazy quilts, embellishments, hand embroidery, surface design techniques, and eventually, art quilts.

I looked for a magazine on the newsstands that was dedicated to art quilting and couldn't find one. I decided to put my doctoral degree on hold and start my own magazine. I named it *Quilting Arts* because I wanted it to celebrate all kinds of artistic styles in quilting—abstract, portraiture, landscapes and nature scenes, and the like—and I wanted to go into detail about design, art quilt construction, tips and tutorials for machine and handstitching, embellishment techniques, and quilting with mixed media.

I can't believe it's been ten years since I founded *Quilting Arts* magazine. As the cliché goes, time has flown. I remember sitting by myself all those years ago in my in-laws' sheep barn with a laptop and a folding table and just the seed of an idea for a magazine in my head. I asked a handful of dedicated friends and people I'd met on quilting message boards online—who thankfully understood the vision—to pitch in and write articles, though I couldn't afford to pay them at the time. I consulted with a publishing guru to help form a business plan, find a printer, and learn all of the ins and outs of magazine publishing to get *Quilting Arts* on its feet.

Since then, I've been fortunate to interview and work with some of the world's most talented contemporary quilters and fiber artists. With this book you'll find the best of the best from the last ten years of our cherished publication—everything from quilt design, fabric collage, and construction to unique surface design application and embellishment techniques. If you want to learn or improve your machine stitching, talented and award-winning quilters offer their advice and tips to make free-motion stitching and thread painting easy, fun, and beautiful. If you are at all like me and thoroughly enjoy painting, dyeing, and screen printing your fabrics (or if you're ready to try your hand at these things), there are plenty of inspiring ideas in the pages ahead. And if you want to spice up your quilts with mixed-media techniques and applications, there are plenty of out-of-the-box ideas for you, too.

It is my hope that this book will provide you with plenty of inspiration and further you on your creative journey.

Pokey Bolton

Founder and Editorial Director
Quilting Arts

Starting and Finishing

art quilt basics

WE CHOOSE TO MAKE ART QUILTS (rather than traditional quilts) because we want to express our point of view with fabric and thread. With so many methods, tools, and techniques at our disposal, sometimes it's difficult to choose the best approach, let alone get started. This chapter will help you transform the quilts that you imagine into real art quilts, with ideas for getting past creative blocks, playing with color, and learning the fundamentals of machine quilting. And what about unique finishing methods? Do you have to apply a traditional binding? Of course not! It all begins right here.

Frieda Anderson, *Dancing Trees* 31" × 27" (79 × 68.5 cm)

Leaf Light
53" × 56"
(134.5 × 142 cm)

Releasing Creative Blocks

Melody Johnson

MAYBE THIS HAS *HAPPENED TO YOU*. Time has been freed up to work in your studio, but when you get down to business, all your ideas are gone or, worse, that great idea you had now seems just mediocre. Feeling slightly desperate, you clean, hoping that a clean studio will lead to creativity. Organization and cleanliness help, but still, where is that wonderful concept for the quilt that you now have time to start? Drinking a cup of coffee, flipping through magazines, pulling out fabric, discovering unfinished projects, feeling guilt about not finishing that hopeless piece, wasting your precious studio time—this is all misery-making. Soon you find yourself declaring that you are in an artistic drought and you sit there in a funk, uninspired.

It is at this point that I begin whining to my husband. If I whine long enough he will offer his standard advice. This is advice that I have heard before, since it is his favorite phrase, one that never goes out of style and fits all situations:

"Get back to basics," he says.

"Ugh!" I say.

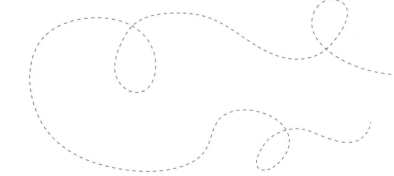

Lollipop Series #4 16½" × 16½" (42 × 42 cm)

Trudging back to the studio, I begin scrounging around under piles of stuff until I find my good old sketchbook. Relief and hope surge through my being. My sketchbook has safely preserved my doodles, drawings, and scribbles from those days when ideas were flowing fast and loose. I review the initial drawings that actually led to finished work and see others that seemed useless at the time but now appear to be evidence of genius!

Turning a page, I discover a doodle that is so simple and elegant that the dam bursts and, voilà, I am carried away, out of the desert and into the realm of possibilities. All things have become clear to me. A block does not have to be square.

Keep a Sketchbook

Even if you think you can't draw, a doodle or diagram is all you need to record a great idea. Bring your sketchbook with you in the car, on the plane, on vacation, or to work, for whenever you have waiting time. One never knows when an idea will reveal itself. If you have a sleepless night, get up and draw. When you visit museums, galleries, or art shows, be sure to collect postcards and brochures, or take photos, if allowed; keep these in your sketchbook for future reference. Analyze the art and grow your own ideas.

MAKE YOURSELF DOODLE

Your subconscious holds ideas that you are unaware of in your conscious mind, and doodling brings them to the surface.

Try this, for example: Draw a shape and then divide the space within that shape. Make all your lines uneven or curved, breaking free from rigid thoughts. Don't be concerned with the difficulties of construction. Simplify, and solutions will be found.

In my sketchbook, my un-square block is composed of a distorted rectangle cut in half, with an oval shape in the middle **(Figure 1)**.

In **Figure 2**, my rectangle-with-oval is paired with simple strips of multiple colors. The center line is thickened into a shape.

DRAW VARIATIONS

Here, variations in size and repeated shapes offer more possibilities. I refer to this as a compound block set.

Vary the size, direction, and number of blocks. Add a simple connecting element or trace a mirror image. Make a big major block and support it with related shapes or mini versions of the same block.

SHADE FOR VALUE

Using your pencil, darken the shapes that need definition. The lines in your drawing can be strengthened and turned into shapes themselves. Trace your original sketch and try alternate versions. Remember that contrast can bring out the best in your quilt. Try to use at least five values, from very light to very dark. Create drama with contrast.

CHOOSE YOUR COLOR SCHEME

Break out of your routine and use that fabric that you have been saving for something important. Delicious fabric makes the quilt much more exciting. Let the fabric do the work for you.

Make a Study

A study can be small and satisfying and can lead to bigger and better versions once the ideas are nurtured and allowed to grow. It need not be complicated to be wonderful. Again, simplify.

BEGIN WITH A LAYOUT

Layout is very important. Sketch possible arrangements in your sketchbook to work out a construction plan.

My favorite method of construction for my wall quilts is fusing, so all those difficult shapes that I have sketched are really quite simple to bring to life. Fusing eliminates the need to turn under edges, include seam allowances, or fit shapes into shapes. Any shape that can be drawn can be cut and fused from fabric.

If your idea is something that can be made traditionally, then you can work out the construction method in the study, saving time and precious fabric for the final masterpiece.

Are you ready? Go release your chains! ■

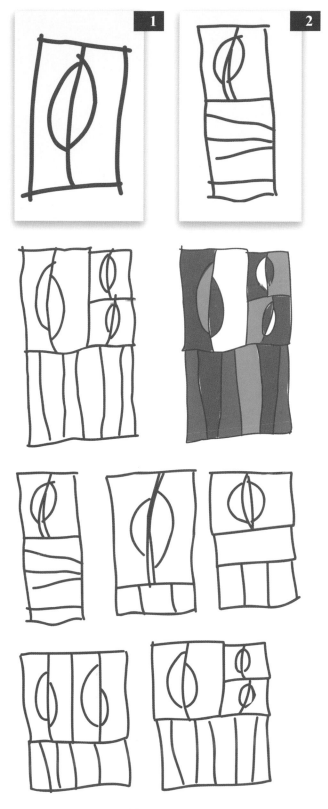

Variations

All the Right Moves

Successful Free-Motion Quilting

Frieda Anderson

BACK IN 1984, I started a king-size Ocean Waves quilt for my sister's second marriage. It was machine-pieced and handquilted. She didn't receive it until after her third divorce. At that time, I realized I needed a quicker way to finish quilting my quilts, so I started machine quilting. When I began machine quilting, I started right in on a queen-size quilt. I did mostly stitch-in-the-ditch and outline quilting around the elements of the block patterns I was making. But I soon branched out and started doing basic stippling. When I got bored with that, I began to do allover free-motion quilting, which is quilting without marking designs first, creating my own and copying any free-motion designs that I saw.

I learned mostly by trial and error, looking at other people's machine-quilted quilts, then going home and trying to duplicate what I had seen. I take a lot of photographs when I go to quilt shows, and I am still always looking for new ideas. Here are a few simple tactics that will help you to be more successful with free-motion machine quilting.

Whispering Pines (detail)
36" × 24"
(91.5 × 61 cm)

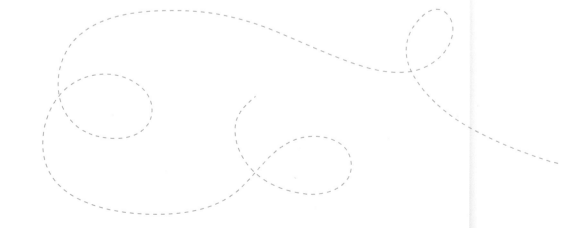

Tall Trees 50" × 50" (127 × 127 cm)

Getting Started

There are five basic elements that will make machine quilting more enjoyable for you.

1 BASIC EQUIPMENT

A sewing machine with the ability to drop the feed dogs is essential. You cannot do free-motion machine quilting well if the feed dogs on your machine does not drop. You can cover up the throat plate, but that creates drag, one of our biggest enemies. If your machine does not have feed dogs that drop, treat yourself and buy a new machine.

You'll need a darning or embroidery foot for your machine. Most machines come with one, but you might want to purchase a clear one that has the front of the foot open, making it easier to see where you are going as you stitch.

I recommend a single-needle throat plate for your sewing machine. This has a smaller hole (relative to a wide one that allows zigzag stitching) where the bobbin thread comes up. This creates a smoother and flatter surface for the quilt to glide over.

Get an adjustable chair, such as an office chair, that allows you to sit up high and look down on your quilting. You should be able to rest your arms on your sewing table surface. You don't want to have to hold your arms up while machine quilting—you will get tired very fast, and that will affect your quilting.

2 THE RIGHT NEEDLE

There are several kinds of sewing machine needles that work well; be sure to use the one most appropriate for your fabric and thread. This can make a big difference in both the appearance and ease of your quilting. These are the four needles I use the most:

Quilting needle. This needle is designed to work through multiple fabric layers and across intersecting seams. Use with cotton quilting thread.

Embroidery needle. This needle has a large eye and special scarf (groove above the eye) to protect decorative threads from shredding or breaking. This needle is good for use with rayon and acrylic fabrics and threads.

Microfiber/Sharp. This needle is best for silks, microfibers, and for penetrating densely woven fabrics.

Metallic. This needle has a specially coated eye that accommodates metallic thread flow at all stitch speeds. A large groove in the shaft protects the thread and helps prevent shredding.

3 THREAD

The thread you use will give your work a distinct look, so experiment. Use a lighter-weight thread in your bobbin than in the needle to help keep the bobbin thread in the middle of the quilt sandwich where it belongs (if you're using a thin thread in the top, then the bottom thread weight should match what is on the top). Remember, the thicker the thread, the smaller the number. The weight of the thread is printed on the spool.

I use a heavier weight thread such as a 30 in my top thread, but I always use at least a 50- or 60-weight thread in the bobbin. Again, experimentation is the key. I also match the color of the bobbin thread to the top thread.

4 FLAT WORK SURFACE

You'll need a flat surface for your quilt to rest on as you work. I have an area that surrounds my sewing machine that is flat for at least 24" (61 cm) and extends all around the sewing surface of my machine.

A flat work surface is especially important when you're working on larger quilts. Drag happens very easily when your project rests on different heights, so the surface all around you should be the same height as your sewing surface.

Drag will cause you to be jerky in your motion and will create tension in your shoulders and arms. Your arms should be supported and relaxed. Your arms should rest on your sewing surface as you use your hands like a hoop to move the quilt around. Avoid pushing or pulling the fabric through the needle, but rather move the fabric under the needle, like paper under a pencil.

I position my hands on either side of an area no larger than a dinner plate, and by grasping the quilt on either side I move the quilt around. When the area I'm working on is full, I reposition the quilt and my hands and start quilting again in a new area. I try to work my quilting away from myself. This allows me to see where I am going. It isn't always possible, but it is a general principle to help you be more successful while free-motion quilting. Roll your large quilts so that they will fit nicely as a package inside the arm of the machine.

5 PRACTICE

The fifth and most important factor in successful machine quilting is quite simple: practice, practice, practice. You cannot get any better if you don't quilt! Have a positive attitude and work hard; you'll succeed. There are many machine-quilting books out on the market; read them for ideas and tips. Don't just look at the pictures, but read them and try some of the exercises in the books. Everyone brings their own quilting expertise and has some little trick that you might find is just the thing you need.

Only by experimentation and practice can you discover what works best for you. The more comfortable you are with your quilting and your setup, the better you will become. Keep quilt sandwiches by your sewing machine to practice on. I always make a small sandwich of the fabric that I have in a quilt, and I use that sandwich to try out threads and needles and patterns before I begin quilting on my finished quilt.

A Pattern for Success

Following are some basic patterns for you to create. By starting with simple shapes and moving into more complex designs, you can learn to draw with thread, just like drawing with a pencil, using free-motion machine quilting to quilt your creations.

Develop a rhythm between your hands and your foot to make smooth stitches. Strive for consistency. By moving your hand to the speed of the needle, you will make clean, smooth stitches.

Sun Dance 28" × 26" (71 × 66 cm)

stars   *triangles*   *feathers*

If you are having trouble working a design without a pattern to follow, draw out your design on a piece of paper and place the paper on your sewing machine without thread in the machine. Practice going around the pattern.

Start out making small quilted projects and work up to larger ones. Go beyond stippling. To do this, you need to be able to create good pivot points and sharp, tight right angles that are not rounded and wimpy. I often find that I count to myself as I work a design. By counting out, I know when to change direction.

Start Quilting

Okay, let's start quilting. Keep these things in mind when you begin:

Bring the bobbin thread to the top of your quilt. Hold your bobbin thread and top thread in your left hand and press down on the presser foot of your sewing machine. After you have started moving, release the thread and with your left hand grab the fabric. Later, tie a square knot with the starting thread and bury it in the same hole it came out of in the quilt sandwich, pulling the knot tight to make it pop into the sandwich.

Start out at a steady speed with the machine, one that you can control. Visualize the design you wish to make. Start moving the fabric under the needle to create the design. Move your hands at the same speed as your foot is making the needle move. Try to always work your pattern away from you. Look ahead to where you are going.

Think about spacing. No matter what the size or shape of the design, consistent spacing creates the best look and allows you to change designs while you are quilting.

Try not to let the needle go up and down in one place as this will create knots on the back of your work.

Work back and forth and up and down, filling in an area about the size of a dinner plate. When you can no longer move the fabric comfortably, stop. If you have the option of needle-down on your sewing machine, use it. If not, when you stop, put the needle in the down position. Readjust the quilt and your hands and then begin to quilt again.

Shapes to Try

SQUARE STIPPLING. Turn your rounded stippling into squares. Make your corners crisp and clean; just keep moving. You can also stitch triangles and stars. Inevitably someone in my machine-quilting classes asks if it is okay to cross lines while machine quilting. It's okay as long as it is part of the design.

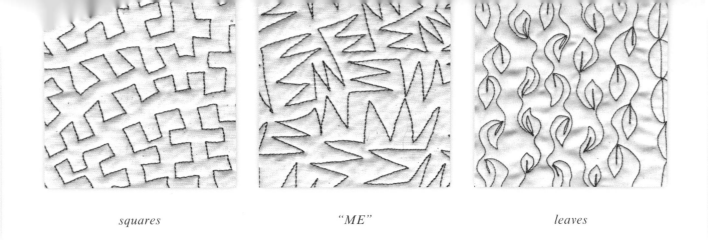

squares　　　　　　　　*"ME"*　　　　　　　　*leaves*

ME, ME, ME. It's all about me. This is my friend Laura Wasilowski's favorite pattern: a series of Ms and Es. The pivot point is very important in this allover design.

LEAVES. All kinds of leaf shapes can be made very easily with free-motion quilting. Link them together with lines, cluster them on top of each other, or connect them top to bottom.

FEATHERS. Stitch feather shapes from the outside in. I tell my students to think of big Roger Rabbit ears—make them floppy and hang over a little. If you don't make the ears floppy, you will make hearts. Hearts are okay, but for feathers you need floppy. Leave a little space between the feathers for a different-looking design.

Tips

- To help the quilt sandwich slide smoothly over the surface of your sewing area, use spray sizing when you iron the backing of your quilt.

- Use Clover Non-slip Finger on your hands instead of gloves. This keeps your fingers tacky so you hold the fabric better.

- Try different battings, making samples and quilting them to see how you like them. At big quilt shows you can often buy small samples from batting vendors.

- Change your needle often. Most needles only last for about eight hours of sewing time.

- Keep your sewing machine clean and oiled. Get in the habit of cleaning your machine after each project. Remove the needle plate from your machine and clean out any lint. Follow the directions in your manual.

- Have your machine serviced at least once a year by a reliable dealer.

- Keep your machine covered when you are not using it. Dust and animal hair are a sewing machine's worst enemies.

modern baptist fan   *traditional baptist fan*   *individual motif*

Georgy Porgy Puddin in Pie **36" × 24"** (91.5 × 61 cm)

clusters I   *clusters II*   *clusters III*

More Free-Motion Stitching Shapes to Try

CLUSTERED DESIGNS Almost any shape can be clustered. Go from making very simple clamshell designs into bigger, bolder flower shapes. Just start a new design on either side of the shape you just finished.

MODERN BAPTIST FAN The traditional version of this motif looks very rigid and straightforward, but you can throw in a few curves and variations to create a modern version of an old favorite.

INDIVIDUAL MOTIFS This is one place you might want to actually mark your designs on the surface of the quilt. I use chalk or soapstone to mark individual designs on the surface of my quilts and use a damp cloth to remove the marks after I've finished stitching. I usually surround individual motifs with simple stippling or filler designs.

As you continue to work at your quilting, remember it takes lots of practice. Look all around you for inspiration—study the machine quilting on the exhibited quilts when you attend quilt shows, read books, take classes, and watch for designs in your everyday surroundings. ■

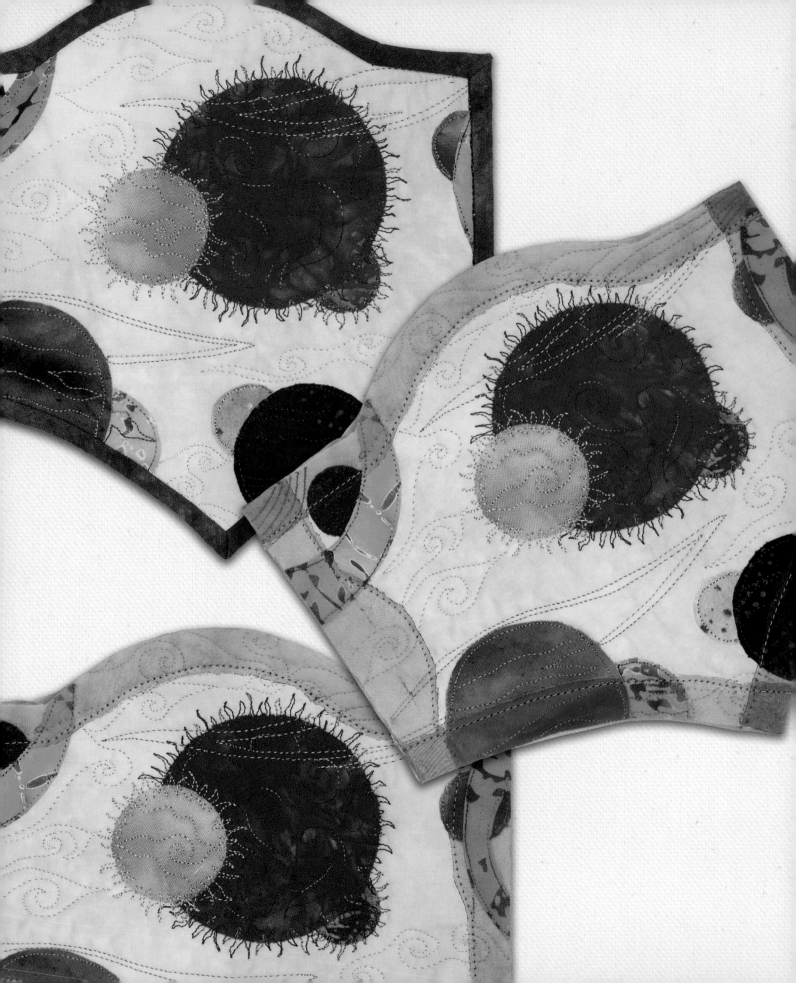

On the Edge

Beautiful Binding Methods

Sarah Ann Smith

"WHAT IF" may be the most useful phrase in an artist's vocabulary. What if I used a pillowcase back instead of a bias binding? What if I used a sheer fabric instead of cotton or silk? What if I stitched an accent line inside the bias binding? In this article, we'll look at several options for finishing quilt edges.

Sometimes one alternative is clearly better looking or more suitable to the intended use of the piece, but other times the best solution is what looks best to you. *Make visual decisions visually.*

When your quilt is nearly finished, set out your fabric and fiber options and really look at them. Will you leave the edges raw with the batting artfully hanging out, perhaps painted? Will you enclose the edges? If your quilt is designed for the wall, you can use any edge finish (or lack thereof) you want. If you are making a garment or bed/lap quilt, you'll want a durable finish that will stand up to washing and the wear and tear of use.

The mini-quilts by Sarah Ann Smith, opposite, illustrate most of the binding challenges you will face, including standard edges and corners, inside and outside curved edges, and points.

Double-Fold Bias Binding

The double-fold bias binding with a mitered corner is probably the most familiar edge finish for contemporary quilts. For demonstration purposes, I created a mini-quilt that illustrates most of the challenges you will face. The sample quilt includes standard edges and corners, inside and outside curved edges, and a point. To bind a curved edge smoothly, you must use binding strips cut on the bias (cut on a 45-degree angle to the woven edge) because bias stretches and can be shaped around curves. The narrower the binding, the easier it is to get it smooth and flat, especially on curves. A double-fold bias binding will wear substantially longer than one cut on the straight of the grain, so it's good for projects that will get a lot of use.

MAKING THE STRIP

1 Cut your binding strips six times the width of the desired finished binding, plus ¼" (6 mm). For a binding that finishes at ⅜" (1 cm) you will need 2⅜" (6 cm) wide strips.

2 Sew your binding strips end-to-end, using diagonal seams with a ¼" (6 mm) seam allowance, until you have a strip the length of your quilt perimeter plus several inches.

3 Fold the strip in half lengthwise, finger-pressing or *lightly* pressing with an iron.

ADDING THE BINDING

1 Align the binding raw edges with the quilt raw edge and, using a ¼" (6 mm) seam allowance, sew the binding to the quilt, beginning at least 4" to 6" (10 to 15 cm) from a corner, and leaving a tail of about 4" to 6" (10 to 15 cm). On large quilts, leave a tail of about 12" (30.5 cm). When stitching is about 2" (5 cm) from the corner, place a pin to mark ¼" (6 mm) from the corner. Stitch up to the pin and backstitch. Remove the pin. Remove the quilt from the machine and cut the threads **(Figure 1)**.

2 Fold the binding up to make a 45-degree angle **(Figure 2)**.

3 Fold the strip back down (covering the 45-degree fold). Align the new fold with the edge of the quilt and align the strip with the next side of the quilt. Starting at the corner, stitch down the next side **(Figure 3)**. Repeat at the remaining corners.

4 Stop stitching about 4" to 6" (10 to 15 cm) from where you began; backstitch. Remove the quilt from the machine and cut the threads **(Figure 4)**.

JOINING THE TAIL ENDS AND FINISHING

1 Press under a ⅜" (1 cm) seam allowance on the beginning tail. Tuck the ending tail inside the beginning tail. Allowing a ½" to 1" (1.3 to 2.5 cm) overlap, trim away the excess **(Figure 5)**.

2 Refold the beginning tail so the ending tail is tucked inside; pin. Finish the seam **(Figure 6)**.

3 Turn the binding to the back. Fold the mitered corners in opposite directions on front and back to balance the bulk.

4 Blindstitch the binding to the back using an invisible hand-appliqué stitch or stitch in the ditch from the front. Blindstitch the join.

The Pillowcase Technique

There are two ways to turn a quilt with a pillowcase backing:

LEAVE AN OPENING along one side. After turning the quilt right side out, turn under the edges of the opening and stitch the opening shut.

USE THE ESCAPE-HATCH method: slice an opening in the center of the back. Handstitch or fuse the opening shut, as described in the following instructions.

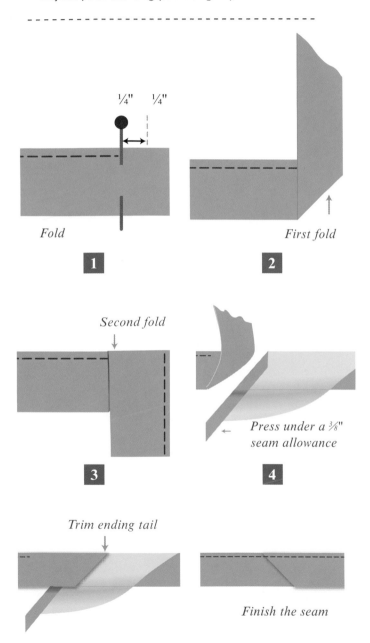

¼"   ¼"

Fold

First fold

1

2

Second fold

Press under a ⅜" seam allowance

3

4

Trim ending tail

Finish the seam

5

6

1 Complete all work on the quilt top. Cut batting the same size as (or slightly larger than) the quilt top and do most or all of the quilting (a piece of cloth under the batting is optional).

2 Trim the quilt top and batting, allowing for a ⅜" (1 cm) seam allowance for the "roll" toward the quilt back.

3 Cut the backing exactly the same size and shape as the top.

4 Trim ⅛" (2 mm) from all edges on the backing. If you will be using the escape-hatch method, apply fusible web to a section of the back and cut the opening now.

5 Place the backing on the quilt, right sides together, and sew along the outside edge using a ¼" (6 mm) seam allowance, easing the top and slightly stretching the back to fit.

6 Trim away as much batting as you can from the seam allowance.

7 Trim the outside corners, as shown below, to reduce bulk when turned. Clip all inside curves and cut notches in all outside curves. Clip into inside corners. Avoid clipping into the stitched seam. If the fabric is raveling a lot, use a short stitch length to reinforce the seam and use a no-fray product where the clips approach the stitching.

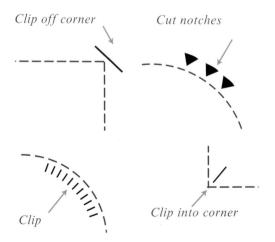

Clip off corner

Cut notches

Clip

Clip into corner

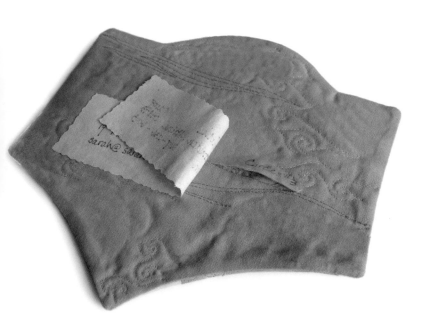

For a quick and easy finish, try the escape-hatch method of the pillowcase technique. The opening is fused closed, then hidden under the label.

8   Turn the quilt right side out. Use a point turner, blunt-tipped large knitting needle, or a crochet hook to ease corners.

9   Iron the seam allowances toward the center of the quilt as follows. Roll just a smidgen of the front edge of the quilt to the back; this is called favoring the edge. From the side, you won't see the backing/facing, so it creates a clean, professional finish to the edge of your quilt or garment. Use an up-and-down (not sliding) motion with a dry iron to set the seams in place.

---

10 Stitch the side opening or escape hatch closed (or fuse it). If the backing is fusible, iron it now. You may wish to add some quilting or stitching to keep the backing in place, especially if your quilt backing is not fused.

11 Sew or fuse your label over the escape hatch to hide the slash.

Sheers

Quilts bound with sheer ribbon are lovely, but ribbon can be expensive, of poor quality, or difficult to find. I developed a method of using sheer synthetic fabrics to finish the edges, providing a subtle visual stop, yet allowing the viewer to see the composition extend all the way from edge to edge. I use a heat tool to cut and sear the edges because sheers fray a lot. You can also rotary-cut these strips and allow the edges to fray or use tulle (netting) or stretch mesh, which will not fray. Because this piece has curves, I cut my strips on the bias. For a quilt with straight sides, you may cut the sheers on the straight grain. Because sheers can be fiddly, I use a wrapped corner instead of a mitered corner.

1. Rotary-cut binding strips at least 2" (5 cm) wider than the desired width. For a ½" (1.3 cm) edge, cut strips 2½" to 3" (6.5 to 7.5 cm). Cut a separate strip for each side of the quilt (cut the strip 2" [5 cm] longer than the quilt side).

2. Fold the binding strip in half lengthwise and insert the quilt, easing the binding fabric until it is snug against the raw edge of the quilt; pin. Repeat on the opposite side **(Figure 1)**.

- -

Tip: Spray baste the inside of the sheer to make pinning easier.

- -

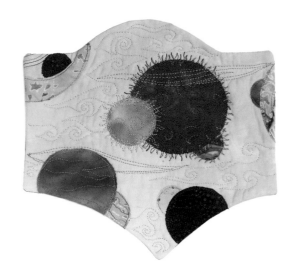

3. Topstitch the binding in place, sewing ½" (1.3 cm) from the quilt's raw edge, then trim the ends of the binding strips flush with the quilt.

4. Trim away the excess width of the binding strip on both the front and the back of the quilt. First, secure your quilt to an ironing surface by pinning on both sides of the stitching line, stabbing the pins through the binding and underneath the excess fabric. Carefully lift the excess fabric and cut or sear the excess away, leaving ⅛" (2 mm) beyond the stitching **(Figure 2)**.

- -

Tip: If you sear too close to the stitching, your sheer may pull loose and threads may melt. Practice on a scrap and on the back side of the quilt before working on the front. Keep your heat tool somewhat vertical or you may melt the binding with the hot shaft of the tool.

- -

Position binding strips on the final two sides of the quilt, pinning from the middle and working outward. Trim the excess binding strip length, leaving ½" (1.3 cm) extending at each end for wrapping to the back of the quilt.

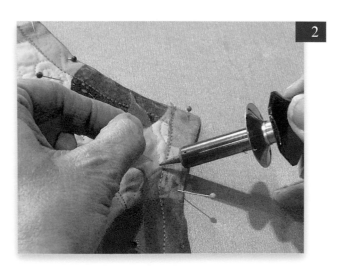

5 Wrap the ½" (1.3 cm) excess strip length to the back and fold it up on the back. Repeat on the other end.

6 In the same manner as above, topstitch and trim away the excess binding strip width.

Wrap-and-Tuck Method

With the wrap-and-tuck method, the backing is wrapped around to the front, so select a backing that will make a nice frame for the front. The wrap method solves two challenges presented by highly irregular quilt edges. First, it provides stability to design elements that extend beyond the quilt top. Second, because it creates a straight line across the top, it is much easier to add a sleeve and hang the quilt.

- -

Tip: Decide on this technique before you have finished quilting. Leave ½" (1.3 cm) unquilted all around the outside edge so there is room to tuck the fabric under the quilt top.

- -

1 Cut the backing and batting oversized. The excess required depends on how far any poking-out bits extend beyond the central background; see Steps 2 and 3. Layer and baste your quilt sandwich. Complete most of the quilting, leaving at least ½" (1.3 cm) unquilted around the edge of the central design.

2 Trim the batting into a rectangle so that all the poking-out bits are supported by batting.

3 Trim the backing, ensuring that it extends far enough beyond the edge of the batting to wrap over the exposed batting and tuck underneath the quilt top, with at least ¼" (6 mm) tucked under the innermost part of the quilt top.

4 Fold opposite sides of the backing inward, wrapping it smoothly around the edge of the batting and tucking it underneath the quilt top; press the folds.

5 Fold the corners to create miters; press.

6 Fold the remaining sides inward; tuck under the quilt top and press the folds.

7 Pin, baste, glue, or fuse the edge of the quilt top to the wrap, making sure the corners stay nicely mitered.

8 Complete the quilting. Be sure to quilt the new frame and the poking-out bits.

- -

Tip: You can dress up the edges where the wrap tucks under the top with satin stitching, couched yarns, embroidery, beads, or other decorative details.

- -

Satin Stitching

Satin stitching, a tightly packed zigzag stitch, is a familiar stitch used in many fabric postcards and artist trading cards; it works as an edge finish on larger pieces as well. It can be tricky to get a dense, professional result, but with practice, satin stitching offers a pleasing edge-finish option. I make two to three rounds of stitching to cover an edge. For the first round, a narrow width and somewhat open-length zigzag is used to secure the three layers of the quilt. I use wider, tightly packed stitches for the subsequent rounds.

1 Starting with your quilted sandwich, secure the quilt top and backing fabrics to the batting along the edges of the quilt by fusing it, or use wash-away tape. This is not necessary if your quilt top is fused and/or densely quilted—every ¼" (6 mm) or closer along the edges. If the fabric isn't secured to the batting, it may lift up or wiggle out from under the satin stitching.

2 Make test samples using different threads and stitch settings and experiment with wash-away stabilizers.

- -

Tip: Do a test to be sure the stabilizer will wash away completely.

- -

3 An open-toe embroidery foot has an area scooped out underneath to permit dense stitching to pass through smoothly and allows you to see what you are doing. If possible on your machine, reduce the presser-foot pressure just a little; or use a free-motion quilting foot, but keep the feed dogs up. The front-to-back motion of the feed dogs helps you keep an even line with free-motion zigzagging.

4 ROUND 1 If you are using a wash-away stabilizer, place a strip under the edge. Use a narrow width and somewhat open length zigzag to secure the three layers of your quilt. On the featured quilt, I used a 2.5 width and a 2.0 stitch length for this round.

5 ROUND 2 Set your machine to the desired stitch width and length. In this case, using a 40-weight Rainbows trilobal polyester thread from Superior Threads, I used a 3.5 stitch width and a .35 length—even shorter than for a buttonhole. If you use a fine thread, such as regular 50-weight sewing cotton, your stitch length may need to be even shorter.

6 CORNERS Stitch up to the end of the corner (or poking-out bit), pivot with the needle on the outside corner, then make sure to overcast the previous stitching. When possible, I try to do a few stitches on the diagonal to create a mitered look and fully cover the corner.

7 CURVES There are two ways to turn satin-stitched curves: needle down pivot and on the fly. Try both and see which works best for you.

a NEEDLE-DOWN PIVOT. Most appliqué books teach the pivot method. Stop with the needle in the down position along the outside (convex) edge of the curve, lift the presser foot slightly and pivot the piece so that your satin stitch will slightly overlap previous stitching. Repeat until the curve is rounded.

On this piece, I painted the edges of the branches instead of stitching them.

b ON THE FLY. I get smoother curves when I turn curves on the fly—as I am stitching. I grab the edges of the quiltlet and steer the edge as if I were holding a steering wheel driving down a winding road.

8 Depending on how the edges look after two rounds, do a third round of satin stitching if desired. ■

A Big Finish for Small Quilts

Terry Grant

WHEN I STARTED MAKING FABRIC POSTCARDS and small quilts, I searched for ways to finish the edges neatly. Traditional bindings seemed too heavy for most small pieces.

I liked the look of a zigzagged or satin-stitched edge, but I could never get them to lie flat or look neat, and turning the corners was a problem. The stitching seemed to hang up on the corners, and often the corners would end up being chewed up by the needle pushing the fabric down into the machine.

I wanted a narrow finish, scaled to the size of a small work, and a clean, straight edge. After some trial and error, I developed some strategies that produce a neat zigzag finish for my small pieces.

Small Frog,
Big Pond
9" × 9"
(23 × 23 cm)

materials

Your quilt	Size 5 pearl cotton
Ruler	Matching thread
Fine-point permanent marker	Sharp scissors
Sewing machine with zigzag stitch	

Green Beans 4" × 6" (10 × 15 cm)

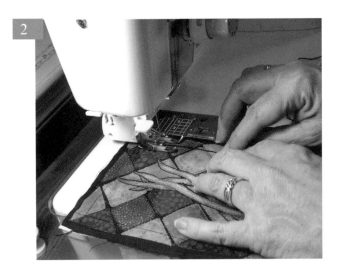

1 Start by making the piece larger than you intend the finished size to be. I like to start with a piece that is ½" to 1" (1.3 to 2.5 cm) bigger in all directions than the finished size.

2 After the piece is quilted, use a ruler and a permanent marker to mark the final size on the top of the quilt **(Figure 1)**.

3 Leaving about ½" (1.3 cm) of floss loose at the beginning, lay a piece of pearl cotton on the marked line and zigzag over it. Use a narrow zigzag that just covers the width of the pearl cotton. Do this before you cut the edges off. Hold the pearl cotton taut against the marked line as you stitch **(Figure 2)**. I use a stitch-width setting of 1.5, and you can leave the stitch length at the default on your machine. You can use a cording foot, but I find turning corners awkward with my cording foot, so I prefer to use my walking foot and carefully stitch over the pearl cotton.

Tip: *It's best not to start and end at a corner. The start and stop are less noticeable along one of the sides.*

----

4 When you get back around to the start of the stitching, cut the pearl cotton so the end butts right up to the start and then stitch over it, taking a few extra stitches beyond the start. The raw ends will be virtually invisible **(Figure 3)**.

5 Carefully trim the excess fabric off, as close to the stitched pearl cotton as you can get without cutting the stitching **(Figure 4)**. If you happen to snip one or two stitches, don't worry. Small errors will be covered later.

6 Using a handsewing needle threaded with a heavyweight thread (I use buttonhole thread), take just one stitch through each corner of your piece. Cut the thread off, leaving two long tails at each corner, each

about 3" (7.5 cm) long. These thread tails will prevent problems when you stitch around the corners.

7   Zigzag over the pearl cotton and the edge again. As you approach a corner, grab the thread tails and use them to guide the stitching up to the corner. Stop with your needle down at the corner, pivot, and use the thread tails to pull the corner gently toward the back, under the foot, while you smoothly stitch into the next straight side **(Figure 5)**. When you are finished, just pull the thread tails out and discard them.

Stitch around the piece several times if you want more coverage. A few stray threads may pop out of the sides. Carefully trim them off. I use black for my edges more often than any other color, as I did for the *Green Beans* postcard, but I have also used other colors, such as the light blue I used for *Small Frog, Big Pond*. Just be sure that your thread color matches the pearl cotton as closely as possible. ■

Color Play

Anne Lullie

MY COLORPLAY MOSAIC quilt series grew from a fascination
with color and the love of a challenge. I have always loved color—
the brighter, the better! I came to a point where I found myself having
"color block," always choosing my favorites or similar colors for my
quilts. I needed what I like to call a colorful intervention. This came
in the form of a quilt show challenge with a color theme. I wanted to
create a rainbow of color in my quilt, but didn't know where to begin.
I decided to go back to the basics, which meant the color wheel.

*Colorplay II
(detail)*
**47" × 51"
(119.5 × 129.5 cm)**

materials

CMY Primary Mixing Wheel
(colorwheelcompany.com)

15" × 17" (38 × 43 cm) hand-dyed
light orange cotton for background

Hand-dyed cotton for color chips,
3" × 14" (7.5 × 35.5 cm) strips in
light, medium, and dark in each
of the following colors: blue (blue
cyan), blue violet (blue), turquoise
(cyan), orange, magenta (primary),
and green (secondary). Use the
CMY color wheel as a guide for
choosing these project fabrics;
the color names in parentheses
match the color wheel.

10" × 20" (25.5 × 51 cm) medium-to-
dark coordinating fabric for binding

Fabric for backing

3 yd (2.75 m) fusible web

17" × 19" (43 × 48.5 cm)
cotton batting

Rotary cutter and mat

Small sharp scissors for
fabric and paper

Tweezers

Iron and ironing surface

Teflon or other pressing sheet

Tray(s) to hold color chips

Prismacolor pencils

Sewing machine

Thread (I use Superior Threads
MonoPoly in clear.)

In my art school days, I had been introduced to the color wheel, and I was fascinated with the color theories of Josef Albers. Simply stated, colors look different depending on the color(s) they are placed next to or on top of. They appear to interact or change their shade or value depending on the colors near them.

With that in mind, I chose light-colored background fabrics and carefully chose color "chips" to appliqué onto them, using the CMY color wheel as a guide. The challenge was to create a design that was visually interesting, using a few basic rules and lots of color. I then fused the chips in place to create the fabric mosaic. I used solid-colored hand-dyed fabrics for the best raw-edge fusing results. The darkest shades create the main design lines, and the medium and light shades (and tints) fill out the design. I found that each new background color sparked new ideas and discoveries, and soon I was hooked on colorplay.

This project begins with an orange background, using the CMY Primary Mixing Wheel to find the corresponding complement, split complement, and tetrad colors. I have included the names of the colors according to the CMY color wheel. If you do not have these exact fabric colors, keep an open mind and use another shade or color. This is all part of the discovery and learning process. This is an excellent project for a hands-on exploration of color. Allow creative freedom with measurements and remember to have fun.

Directions

USING THE CMY COLOR WHEEL

1 Locate Side B on the CMY color wheel. This is the side of the wheel showing the tints and shades (color mixed with black) **(Figure 1)**.

2 Hold the color wheel with the orange section in the 6:00 position.

3 Line up the opening with orange as the key color.

4 The complementary color is at the twelve o'clock position: blue cyan.

5 Note the location of the split complementary and tetrad colors.

FUSING THE FABRIC

Prepare the fabrics listed in the Materials list with fusible web, using a hot iron, no steam (or manufacturer's directions).

1 To fuse the 3" (7.5 cm) fabric strips, place the glue side of the fusible web face up on your ironing surface. Place the strips wrong side down on the fusible's glue side. Overlap the edges of the strips about ⅛" (3 mm). (The overlap will be trimmed off later.)

2 Fuse carefully, picking up the iron and placing it on the next area to be fused. Use the pressing sheet to prevent any fusible from sticking to your iron.

3 Let the fabric cool and then remove the paper backing from all of the fabric strips.

4 With the fusible side of the fabric strips facing up, use a rotary cutter to trim any non-fused edges from the fabric strips.

5 Fuse the orange background fabric to the batting, leaving the excess batting at the edges.

MAKING THE FABRIC CHIPS

1 Using a rotary cutter and mat, cut all of the strips into 1" to 1¼" (2.5 to 3.2 cm) wide strips. Varying the widths adds visual interest.

2 Cut each strip into chips about 1" (2.5 cm). Keep the chips separated by color and shade (lights, darks, mediums) in a tray **(Figure 2)**.

CREATING THE MOSAIC DESIGN LINE

There are several ways to make a guide for the placement of the dark chips.

Colorplay V 25" × 43" (63.5 × 109 cm)

1 Lightly draw a freehand S-curve dotted line from the lower left corner of the orange background to the upper right corner of the background.

2 Alternatively, you can trace the edge of a curved object to draw an S-curve dotted line onto the orange background with a light Prismacolor (or other) pencil or cut a full-size S curve from paper and use it as a guide to place the first two lines of dark color chips (no marking).

THE MOSAIC DESIGN

1 Begin with the dark color chips (dark blue, dark blue violet, dark turquoise, dark

orange, dark magenta, and dark green) and place them along the S-curve design line. Leave a tiny space in between each color chip. Use a variety of the dark colors; do not have two of the same color adjacent to one another.

2 Fuse the dark chips in place with a hot iron.

3 Repeat this process to make a second line of color chips next to the first line, staggering the color chips, like bricks in a wall. Again, use a variety of dark colors, with no two of the same color adjacent to one another **(Figure 3)**.

4 Separate all of the medium color chips from the fabric chips.

5 Repeat Steps 1, 2, and 3 using the medium color chips, placing them in two lines on each side of the dark-colored lines of chips **(Figure 4)**.

6 Use medium color chips to also branch outward from the S curve in straight lines, if desired.

7 Begin to mix light color chips with medium color chips to create additional rows. Finish with light color chips on the outer edges **(Figure 5)**. The chips may extend onto the batting; they will be trimmed later.

FINISHING

1 Add a backing fabric of your choice. This may be fused also.

2 Machine quilt using the method and thread of your choice.

3 Using the rotary cutter and mat, trim the quilt edges straight and then square up the corners.

4 Bind your quilt, using the 10" × 20" (25.5 × 51 cm) medium-to-dark coordinating fabric.

5 Apply a hanging sleeve to the back of the quilt. ■

Colorplay III 52" × 56" (132 × 142 cm)

ART RESOLUTIONS AND GOALS

Jane Dávila

WE OFTEN WAIT until a new year arrives to make resolutions and set goals, but it's something you can do anytime you want to grow as an artist. Now is the perfect time to stop and think about what you'd like to accomplish as an artist and in your art career.

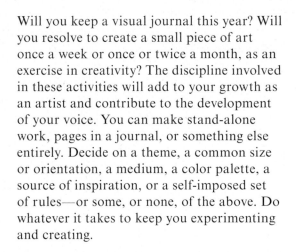

Will you keep a visual journal this year? Will you resolve to create a small piece of art once a week or once or twice a month, as an exercise in creativity? The discipline involved in these activities will add to your growth as an artist and contribute to the development of your voice. You can make stand-alone work, pages in a journal, or something else entirely. Decide on a theme, a common size or orientation, a medium, a color palette, a source of inspiration, or a self-imposed set of rules—or some, or none, of the above. Do whatever it takes to keep you experimenting and creating.

Find Inspiration

You can use an external source to provide inspiration for your visual journaling, such as the word prompts on the Illustration Friday website (illustrationfriday.com). Opportunities for inspiration abound on the Internet; you can find a challenge in almost every media and size. Generally, to participate in these challenges, you create a piece within the challenge guidelines, upload it, and post a link to a blog or photo-sharing site so that other people in the challenge can see what you've done. Try out a variety of sites to see what suits you or jump around as the whim hits you.

Set Goals and Take Steps

Set goals that are realistic; acknowledge what you have control over and what you don't. Break down tasks into steps. Making a list of steps can turn a truly daunting goal into something manageable, and as you achieve each step you'll have the incentive to continue until you've accomplished your goal.

For example, setting acceptance into a prestigious show such as Quilt National as a goal is impractical because you have no control over whether your submission will be accepted. Instead, resolving to *enter* Quilt National is a perfect goal. After you've decided to enter the show, outline the steps you need to take:

Create a piece (or pieces) specifically for the show or determine if any of your existing work is suitable for entry. If you are creating new art, set a deadline to complete the work and adjust your schedule so that you have the time you need.

Learn about high-quality photography, including the equipment you will need and the guidelines the jury requires. Or find a professional photographer who can do this for you (and set up a savings plan to be sure you can afford it).

Mark the submission deadline on a calendar and follow all submission instructions very carefully.

Make Resolutions and Accomplish Them

To feel empowered and motivated to get going, try something my friend Nancy does every January after she makes her list of resolutions: make a list of everything you've made or done, art-wise, for the year that's just ended. You'll be surprised at everything you've accomplished, and this will help you prepare to meet your resolutions head on.

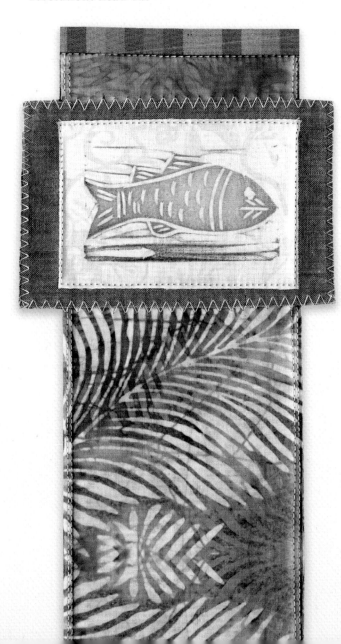

HOW MANY PIECES WOULD YOU LIKE TO COMPLETE THIS YEAR? Determine how many and their approximate sizes (saying small, medium, or large is enough). Look at how you use your time now and what you would need to change to be able to devote the time necessary to meet your art-producing goal.

WOULD YOU LIKE TO LEARN OR MASTER A NEW TECHNIQUE? To do so, would you need to take a workshop, or will meeting your goal require a course of self-study? If you're interested in mastering a technique, you'll need to devote the time to achieve this. Putting in the time with practice is how you get there, so set up a schedule for this practice and stick to it. Periodically stop to assess your progress and see if you'll need to spend more or less time to reach your goal.

IS THIS THE YEAR TO IMPROVE YOUR PROFESSIONAL PRESENCE? Would you like to start a blog or a website? Will you print up business cards and postcards and start submitting work to shows and galleries? Set some specific goals and then make lists of what you'll need to do to achieve them.

After you've made your list of art goals and resolutions for the new year, take stock every month or so to see how you're doing and to keep yourself on track. Feel free to add (or subtract) items as the year goes on. Organizing yourself and your plans is a sure way to help achieve your goals. ■

Trends in Surface Design
stamping, dyeing, printing, and more

CREATING YOUR OWN UNIQUE FABRICS can be a very gratifying and fun process. If you're new to surface design applications, you may think that you need to make a sizable monetary investment to create your own fabrics, but fortunately you don't. Gelatin monoprinting, for example, has only about a $2 cost for gelatin that's readily available in the baking section of your grocery store. Soy wax batik is also a fairly low-cost investment but one of my favorite processes because it makes batik so easy. To apply your own designs to fabric, one of the simplest techniques is Thermofax screen printing—more of an investment, but well worth it! Look for more ideas for stunning surface design in this chapter.

Ana Buzzalino, *The Blue Door* 31" × 28" (79 × 71 cm)

Collagraphs

Monoprinting with Texture Plates

Heidi Miracle-McMahill

THOUGH I ENJOY THE RESULTS of traditional printmaking, I did not like the long processes involved, and I really thought printmaking might not be for me—until I discovered collagraphs. Loosely defined, a collagraph is a print made from a collage. I was fascinated with the idea and wanted to translate the effect to my fiber art. I did some experimenting to perfect my monoprinting, and I learned a few things. My biggest discovery was foam sheets! I started by using the foam for the shapes on a Plexiglas base and quickly discovered that I could use the foam sheet as a base plate as well. I liked the way the foam released the paint, and I liked that I didn't have to wait for any glue or sealer to dry as I had to do with traditional methods.

Construction I
12" × 12"
(30.5 × 30.5 cm)

materials

Foam sheet for printing plate, 9" × 12" (23 × 30.5 cm) or 12" × 18" (30.5 × 45.5 cm)	Brayer
	Iron
Sticky-back foam sheets for cutouts	**optional**
Prepared-for-dyeing (PFD) cotton fabric cut into 15" × 18" (38 × 45.5 cm) or 16" × 24" (40.5 × 61 cm) rectangles	Colored pencils
	Stiff interfacing for batting
Acrylic paints	Embroidery floss
	Gallery-wrapped primed canvas
Small mist sprayer	Pointed tool such as a letter opener
Paintbrushes	

Foam sheets are not the only material I use in my collagraphs, but more often than not I now use a foam sheet as my base plate. It makes the process quick and easy. You can cut shapes to collage onto the plate, and you can draw or etch into the foam itself.

Directions

1 Sketch out your design on paper. I work spontaneously but know that many artists prefer to lay out a design on paper first. Keep it fairly simple; you have to be able to cut out what you have drawn.

2 Cut your desired shapes from the adhesive-backed foam sheets and arrange them on the large foam sheet.

3 When you are happy with the arrangement, begin peeling off the backing and sticking the pieces onto the background sheet. Leave enough space so that you can get your fingers in between the cut-out shapes.

4 Cut a piece of PFD cotton fabric 2" to 3" (5 to 7.5 cm) larger on all sides than your printing plate.

5 Apply paint to your collagraph foam plate using a brush, a brayer, or even your fingers. You can leave white areas, blend areas together, etc.

Tip: Make sure your paint is not too thick or you will get blobby prints on your fabric.

6 Mist your paint just a bit with a fine-mist sprayer. Use only enough mist to keep it wet and to help release the paint without making it runny.

7 Carefully place your dry fabric on top of the plate. Do your best to square it up so that you have a consistent straight border on all sides (much harder than it sounds). Once you lay it down on the paint, it's usually not a good idea to move it.

8 Mist your fabric from the back. Less is more to start with.

9 Use your hands, fingers, and fingernails to gently rub the raised foam areas and the areas around the shapes, being careful not to shift the fabric. Rub around each raised area or section at a 90-degree angle to the foam plate to make clean, crisp edges. This will require pushing the fabric ever so slightly around your shapes, sort of like embossing a shape onto paper. Use any pointed tool that helps you get as close as possible to the edges of your foam cutouts.

Tip: You may see paint color coming through your fabric, but it should not appear to be running or bleeding. If it is, you have used too much water. If you gently lift your fabric and see that the print is not dark enough, you can very carefully lay it back down, mist some more, and rub some more. Or you may find you have not used enough paint and will have to start over.

----

10 Lift your fabric away from the plate, let it dry, and heat-set with an iron.

I love to add even more color and depth to my collagraphs with colored pencils after the paint is dry. I often do some handstitching. I use a stiff interfacing as my batting, and when I finish stitching, I mount the small quilt on a painted canvas. When you are comfortable with foam-sheet printing, move on to other materials on your collagraph plates. Experiment with different textures such as molding paste, sand, leaves, and other organic materials. There is a world of texture to be discovered. ∎

Tips

• Misting the paint just before printing helps the paint to release.

• Laying dry fabric on top of the paint and then misting it from the back prevents bleeding problems.

• Misting rather than wetting the fabric gives you more control.

• Using my hands and fingers to apply pressure to the print plate works better than anything else I tried.

Flight of Fantasy

A Gelatin Monoprint Process

Frances Holliday Alford

SEVERAL YEARS AGO, I spent an afternoon doing gelatin monoprinting with a small group of fellow art quilters. I had a general idea of the process but had never tried it. We each started with a very stiff circular slab of gelatin, stiff enough that light hand pressure did not even dent the surface. Each of us worked in our own way. We added paint to the gelatin surface, or plate, and by gently smoothing fabric over the painted surface, we were able to lift one-of-a-kind monoprints. The paint adhered to the fabric, making an interesting, unique image that could not have been achieved by a direct paint method. It is a process that is spontaneous, creative, and exciting.

We worked all afternoon, and when I left, I had a large stack of circular prints on 12" (30.5 cm) squares of white cotton fabric. I spent the next several days adding color using marking pens and paints. And when the prints screamed for it, I started machine quilting. The edges started ruffling from the tension of the machine stitching and from the extra thread. I liked the three-dimensional forms that this added to the surface design.

Flight of Fantasy (detail)
10" × 10"
(25.5 × 25.5 cm)

materials

Unflavored gelatin	Fabric paints
Water	Fabric markers
Saucepan and measuring cup	Sharpie or Pigma Micron pens
Heat source	Brayer and/or paintbrushes
Pie pans or other round containers	High-loft polyester batting
White cotton fabric	Thread in a variety of colors
Backing fabric	Shiva Paintstiks

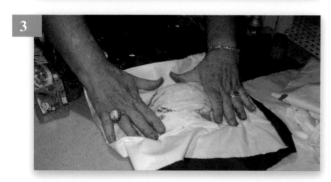

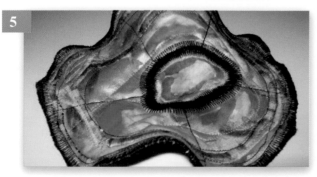

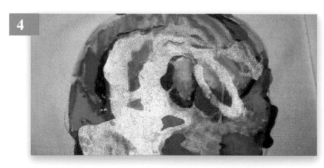

I laid out the forms in a series and found that they could cover a large space, just the right size for the 2006 Husqvarna Viking Imagine That! contest. My entry, *Flight of Fantasy*, was a finalist and traveled for a year throughout Europe. Since then I've enjoyed reminiscing about its creation.

Directions

MAKE GELATIN PLATES

1 Use two envelopes of household gelatin per one cup (237 ml) of water. You will probably need at least four cups (946 ml) of water and eight packets of gelatin for a good-sized plate.

2 Measure the cold water into a large saucepan. Add the gelatin powder and allow it to soften in the cold water.

3 Heat the water and gelatin until it is boiling. Stir regularly, and do not allow it to boil for a long time as it could scorch the gelatin.

4 Remove from heat and stir. When all of the gelatin has dissolved, pour the liquid into pie pans or other round containers **(Figure 1)**. Refrigerate until the gelatin is cool and gelled into a stiff surface. If you want a particular shape, the plate can be trimmed, cut, or carved.

5 Remove from the refrigerator and loosen the edges of the gelatin from the pan. Turn the container over onto a fabric or paper surface and carefully remove the gelatin plate.

6 Let the plate sit for a few minutes to allow it to dry. Otherwise, it will be wet and slick from condensation.

PRINTING

1 With the gelatin plate on a dry, clean surface, apply fabric paint to the surface of the plate with a brayer, a brush, or your hands. You can also just squeeze paint onto the plate, as I did **(Figure 2)**.

2 Lay a piece of white cotton fabric over the painted gelatin plate and smooth the fabric in place, moving from the center out in all directions **(Figure 3)**.

3 Lift the fabric from the plate and allow the fabric to air-dry face up **(Figure 4)**.

4 Add more paint to the plate and continue to make prints or continue to print without adding paint; this is called ghost printing. The second print will be similar to the first, but lighter.

CREATING TEXTURE

Here are several ways to add texture to your monoprint.

- Add an item to act as a mask to the paint below it. Threads or string will prevent paint from adhering and create white lines in the painted surface. Cut paper, leaves, and other flat objects may be used as masks to leave unpainted areas.

- Gouging or breaking your plate gives the piece a different look. Smaller pieces of the plate may be isolated and used as stamping tools by painting on them and applying them directly to the fabric surface.

- An alternative to tearing the gelatin plate is to use a cookie cutter or a knife to make a more formal shape. Cutting into the plate will leave places where extra paint will sit, allowing darker lines to appear on your fabric.

SECONDARY PAINTING AND EMBELLISHMENT OF PRINTS

After the monoprinted fabric is dry, try these enhancements.

- Use fabric markers or direct paint application to enhance the color and design.

- Add Shiva Paintstiks as an accent by rubbing them over a textured surface.

- Create more texture and visual interest with a second pass through the monoprint phase with the gelatin plate.

CONSTRUCTION PROCESS

Construct each piece as a separate unit.

1 Use batting and a backing fabric and lightly pin all three layers together to create a fabric sandwich.

2 Baste the pieces together so that they will not shift during stitching.

3 Using satin stitch (a dense zigzag), sew all around the irregular edges several times. Trim away any excess from the edges of the forms.

4 Free-motion quilt each unit, starting from the center and working out. I found that making satin-stitched spirals from the center out to the edges was an effective way to add bright thread work. I also used straight stitches, radiating from the center, to emphasize the starburst pattern of these forms **(Figure 5)**.

5 When all units are completed, spread them out on a design board with the edges overlapping, and pin the units together.

6 Attach two to three units at a time, using machine stitches that imitate or match the stitching on the edges of the individual units.

7 Continue to attach units until the entire quilt is assembled. No binding is necessary, as the satin-stitched edges of the separate units are already finished.

8 Add a sleeve at the top of the back. By arranging the top row of the quilt carefully, the sleeve may be completely obscured from the front of the piece.

9 Add a label with the title and your contact information, and be sure to sign it.

This process is forgiving, flexible, and spontaneous. There are as many varieties of production as there are artists making art. Each one brings a different color palette, a shift in shape, and variation in stitch patterns, thread colors, and attachment techniques. ■

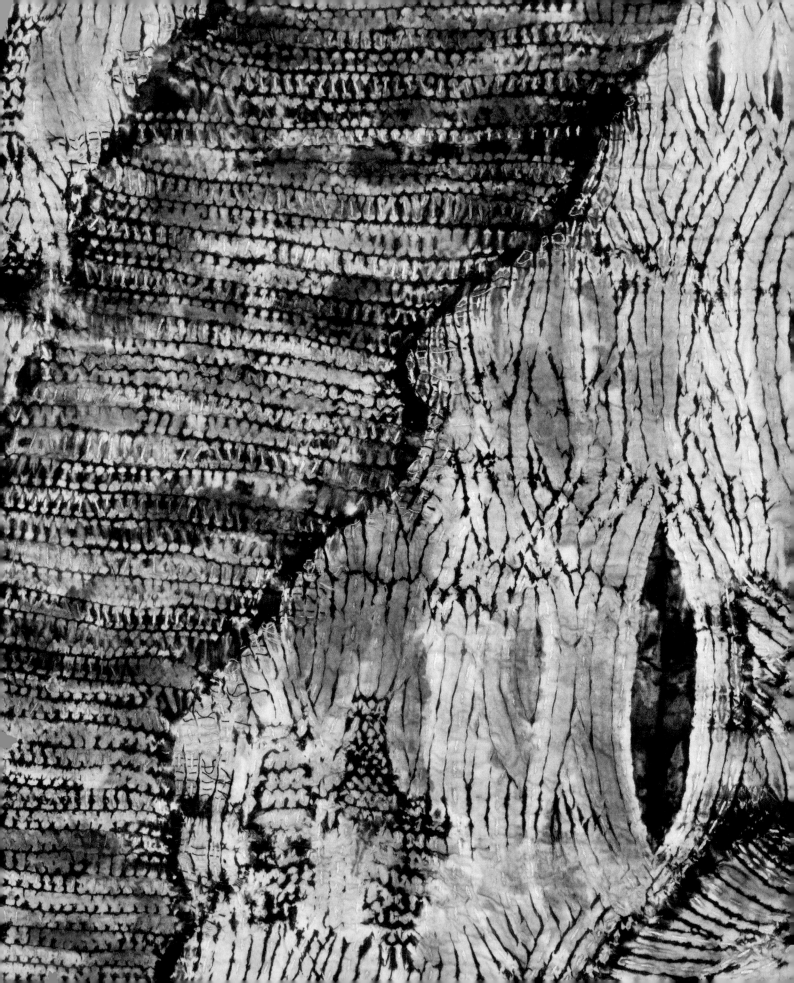

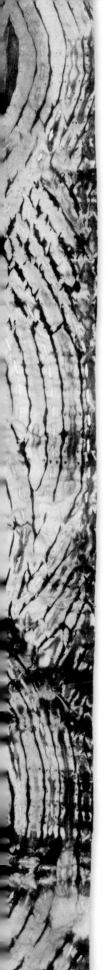

Extreme Shibori

Taking Stitch-Resist Shibori Beyond the Norm

Sue Cavanaugh

WHEN I STARTED dyeing my own fabric, I was especially drawn to stitch-resist *shibori.* Shibori is the Japanese term for various methods of shaped-resist dyeing, including pole wrapping, clamping, folding, and binding. As a lifelong handstitcher, I found the stitches of shibori compelling. I started putting different stitches together to form a pattern and experimented with slight changes to the stitches to alter the pattern. Even as I have greater control of the pattern, I still find that it's the surprise—the part that I can't control—that draws me to this method. The whole-cloth quilt shown here uses an adaptation of the mokume stitch and the *ori-nui* stitch. Mokume means wood grain and is traditionally done in rows of running stitches with no attempt to line up the stitches; this variation allows me to control the direction of the lines. Ori-nui creates a toothlike pattern and is done on the fold in undulating rows with spaces between.

Ori-Kume #5
18" × 18"
(45.5 × 45.5 cm)

materials

A sketch of your choice	Fabric dye, soda ash solution, and other dyeing supplies
Fabric in the desired size of your finished piece	Needle and strong thread or cord
Quilter's marking pencil	Backing fabric and batting

mokume variation

Sketch

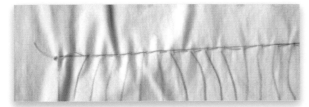
Initial stitching line

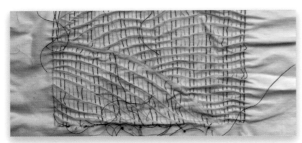
Lines stitched

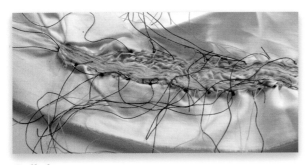
Pulled taut

Painted with dye

All my work starts with a sketch. I look through my sketches and select one that stands out, then explore and refine it until I'm happy with the composition. I then enlarge the sketch on paper to the size I want the finished piece to be and trace the markings onto my cloth.

I like to stitch in the extreme, covering my entire piece of fabric with stitches that result in a pattern. These stitches are pulled tight and knotted before applying the first layer of dye. After batching, the piece is washed and the stitches are removed to reveal the pattern. I then paint the fabric with thickened dyes to add color before quilting the piece. If I want to keep some of the texture, I reverse these last two steps, quilting before adding color. The result is a quilt that has history: stitches next to images formed by stitches that are no longer present.

Directions

1 Select a sketch that pleases you and enlarge it to the desired size of your finished piece.

2 Transfer the sketch to your cloth using a quilter's marking pencil.

3 Stitch your cloth using one of the following stitches, or a combination of the two. Both call for multiple lines of running stitches, each line made with a separate thread. Knot the end of each thread before stitching.

THE MOKUME STITCH VARIATION

Unlike traditional mokume stitching, you control the placement of this stitch by taking

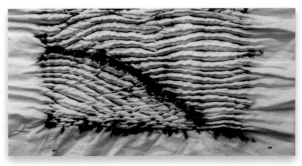
Stitches removed

a small stitch under the sketched line and leaving a longer stitch on top, in between the sketched lines. Note that the stitches run perpendicular to the sketched lines; this will create a pattern that follows the original sketched lines after dyeing.

THE ORI-NUI STITCH

Fold your fabric along each sketched line, and stitch through each fold, distorting the fabric as you stitch. Note that if you stitch horizontally, the primary pattern after dyeing will also be horizontal.

4   Pull the stitches tight so that the fabric is distorted and secure with a square knot. Note that with the ori-nui stitch, the fabric distortion is even greater.

5   Soak the piece in a soda ash solution. Paint dye onto the right side, then wrap the piece in plastic and batch.

6   After twenty-four hours of soaking in the dye and soda ash solution, wash the piece and remove the stitches to reveal the pattern.

7   Paint dye onto the piece to add color.

8   Now you have a beautiful shibori-dyed piece of fabric. Layer your backing fabric, batting, and shibori cloth. Quilt your piece. I like quilting a design that mirrors the original mokume and ori-nui stitches. ■

ori-nui stitch

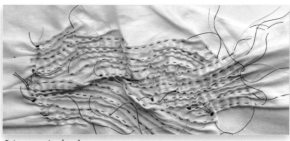
Lines stitched

Pulled taut

Painted with dye

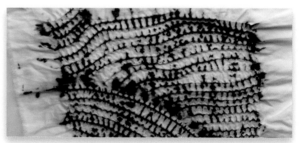
Stitches removed

Initial stitching line

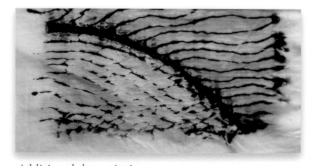
Additional dye painting

Carvum Stampum

Marks of Distinction

Laura Wasilowski

WHETHER YOU'RE USING a simple textural stamp or your own individual typeface, a handcarved stamp makes distinctive marks on paper or fabric. I use my own handcarved stamps for the creation of fabric art as well as cards, calendars, book illustrations, and mail art.

For me there is an art to stamp carving as well as a joy in the act of carving. Although I first made handcarved stamps to create unique designs on the surface of my fabrics, I soon discovered that I enjoyed the act of carving as much as creating new stamps. I carve a stamp, print it once, and then move on to the next stamp.

Stamping in the Sun
11" × 11½"
(28 × 29 cm)

materials

Safety-Kut printmaking block (Staedtler Mars erasers work too, but the stamp size is limited to the size of the eraser.)

X-Acto or Testors craft knife with a #11 blade, or other sharp pointed carving blade

Linoleum block cutters to outline, texture, and remove large areas of stamp material

Paper

#2 pencil

Stamp pad for testing your stamp (choose an ink made for fabric)

optional

Copyright-free image printed from your computer

Cotton balls

Acetone or nail polish remover

TRANSFER THE IMAGE

There are several ways of transferring your image to the stamp's surface before printing; here are three options. For text, use method 2 or 3.

METHOD 1 Draw the image directly onto the Safety-Kut with a pencil or marker. Remember, the image will be reversed when printed.

METHOD 2 To transfer a black-and-white copyright-free image onto Safety-Kut, first cut the stamp block to the approximate size of the image. Place the printed side of the paper onto the Safety-Kut and saturate the paper using a cotton ball with acetone or nail polish remover. Carefully remove the paper and a mirror image of the design will appear **(Figure 1)**.

METHOD 3 Trace the shape of a Safety-Kut block onto a piece of paper. Draw or trace your design within the block's outline using a #2 pencil. Place the pencil side of the drawing onto the Safety-Kut, matching the block to the drawn outline of the block. Rub the lines of the drawing with a fingernail or burnisher. Remove the paper to reveal a mirror image of the design **(Figure 2)**.

CARVE THE STAMP

The object in stamp carving is to remove all the areas of stamp material that you do not want to print onto your fabric or paper. In this simple leaf stamp, we are first removing the center vein, the small dot, and then carving outside of the leaf shape.

1 After drawing or transferring your image onto the surface of the stamp block, determine which areas of the stamp need to be removed. For reference, you can mark or fill in the areas you want to save with a pencil.

2 Place the block on a stable cutting mat and grip the edge of the stamp block with one hand. Make sure your fingers are not in line with the sharp cutting blade.

3 To carve the center vein of the leaf, insert the tip of the knife about $1/8$" to $1/4$" (2 to 3 mm) into the stamp block. As you insert the knife, tilt the blade tip slightly away from the edge you are carving. This slight angle will make the wall of the printing surface stronger so the stamp holds up better. If you're a right-handed person, this means the line you are cutting away from is always on the right side of the blade and the knife angles to the right.

Tip: Always cut away from the edge to be retained; do not undercut this edge.

4 Slowly, keeping the knife tilted, draw the knife blade along the edge of your design. Do not saw at the edge; a nice, even stroke of the blade gives a smooth edge.

5 Rotate the block 180 degrees and insert the knife tip where the first cut ended. Draw the knife down the edge of this vein line. Again, angle the knife. You will carve out a wedge of stamp material.

6 Carve the small circle by placing the tip of the knife into the block at the drawn line. Slowly rotate the block beneath the tip and follow the edge of the line.

7 Remove the excess materials on the outside edges of the leaf design using the same wedge removal method as in Steps 4 and 5.

Tip: Practice shifting and pivoting the block, rather than moving the blade. As you become more proficient you will find that the blade stays almost stationary and the block is guided against the blade with the other hand. This gives a cleaner line and is a more efficient method of carving.

8 Remove large areas outside the design by just cutting them off with the blade. Or, continue to carve away the rest of the stamp material with the wedge removal system. Again, never undercut the design. Linoleum block cutters

can remove the excess in a wider stroke. Steadily push the cutter away from you and your fingers. The advantage of a block cutter is that it has the depth and angle built into the blade.

9 Test the stamp as the design emerges by tamping it onto the stamp pad and printing onto paper. Remove any areas that are picking up unwanted ink and test again. ■

Tips

- Begin by carving the fine details of the design, then move on to removing larger pieces.

- Use linoleum block cutters to create quick cross-hatched textural surfaces and to chip the edges of your stamps for a postage stamp effect.

- For shaped stamps, carve the details of the stamp from a square block, then remove the excess stamp material from the outside edges of the stamp.

- Carve the edges and other side of the stamp, too.

- To attach a handle, glue a wood block to the back of the stamp with E-6000 craft glue.

- Use the sharp end of a copper pipe or tube to cut accurate circles.

- For the really brave, try carving with a Dremel tool!

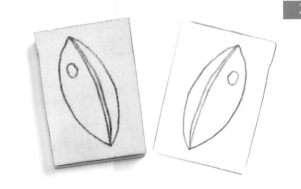

Stamping in the Forest 15" × 7" (38 × 18 cm)

Create with
Discharge Paste

Ana Buzzalino

I HAD READ about discharge paste in *The Painted Quilt*, a book written by Linda and Laura Kemshall. When I was thinking about techniques and ideas to try for the *Quilting Arts* 2010 Calendar Challenge, I decided to give this technique a try. I had some fabric that I had dyed with Procion dyes and thought it would be a good candidate for a little experimentation. The dyed fabric was very bright, with large areas of oranges, greens, and yellows.

Two Pears #2 (detail)
12" × 12"
(30.5 × 30.5 cm)

materials

Fabric dyed with Procion MX dyes	Smock or old shirt to wear
Design of your choice	Plastic sheet to cover work area
Rotary cutter, mat, and ruler	Iron
Freezer paper	Pressing cloth
Paper scissors	Disposable face mask or respirator
Fabric paint in colors of your choice	Mild detergent
Jacquard Discharge Paste	Old towel
Styrofoam tray	Prismacolor colored pencils
1" (2.5 cm) bristle brush or foam brush	Batting
Gloves	Backing fabric
	Quilting thread to match fabric

Two Pears 12" × 12" (30.5 × 30.5 cm)

Jacquard Discharge Paste will remove most fiber reactive colors, direct dyes, and acid dyes from fabric. It is easy to use; just follow the manufacturer's instructions. This paste can be mixed with fabric paint to add color to your work. The discharge paste will remove the color on the fabric and replace it with the color of the paint.

Directions

1 Select a piece of fabric and cut it 1" (2.5 cm) larger on all sides than the desired finished size of your piece. It will be trimmed after quilting. It's a good idea to test your fabric to get an idea of how it will react (see Make a Fabric Sample, opposite).

2 Trace your design onto the dull side of a piece of freezer paper (just the outline is needed).

3 Cut out the major motifs from the freezer paper and iron them (shiny side down) to the fabric, keeping in mind that the area covered by the freezer paper won't discharge (for my quilt, I ironed on freezer paper templates of the pears and table). Be sure

the edges of the paper stick properly to the fabric so the discharge paste doesn't seep under them (**Figure 1**).

4 Cover your work surface. Mix the discharge paste with the fabric paint and apply it carefully and evenly with a wide brush (**Figure 2**). Set the work aside and let it dry.

- -

Tip: Brush away from the freezer paper to prevent lifting it with the brush.

- -

5 Iron the fabric, placing a cloth between the iron and the fabric to protect the iron. Set the iron to the lowest temperature possible with steam. As you iron, you will see the paste/paint mixture starting to react. Once finished, let it cool.

- -

Caution: Be sure to iron in a well-ventilated area as the fumes are quite strong; wear a respirator.

- -

6 Remove the freezer paper (**Figure 3**) and wash the fabric in warm water with a drop of mild soap. Roll the fabric in an old towel to remove as much moisture as possible; iron it dry.

7 When the fabric is dry, lightly separate the different elements of the design with a coloring pencil. The color of the different areas can also be adjusted with additional fabric paint. In *The Blue Door*, page 42, the small pumpkin in front was originally too orange and didn't contrast enough with the other elements in the still life. I used green fabric paint to change the color of the small pumpkin to a greenish tint and used yellow, green, and orange pencils to add highlights and deepen shadows.

When you are happy with the design, layer the piece with batting and backing. Baste or pin to hold the layers in place. Quilt as desired. ∎

Tip: After the quilting is done, you can still adjust the colors of the final piece by using fabric paint and/or coloring pencils. If the colors of two elements are too close, adjust them to better differentiate the elements and create depth.

make
a fabric sample

Cut a small piece of the fabric you are using. If your fabric contains multiple colors, be sure that the piece includes all or most of the colors that will be in your final quilt. Mix a small amount of discharge paste with the fabric paint and paint a section with a brush. Make a note of the ratio of discharge paste to fabric paint as you work. Repeat with different colors and different ratios. Let dry. Iron with steam to allow the discharge paste to react. Wash the fabric and allow it to dry. This sample will give you an idea of what the fabric will look like when you discharge it.

Abstract
Digital Imagery

Connie Rose

FOR THE LAST COUPLE OF YEARS, I've experimented widely with digital imagery on fabric, trying different techniques and materials in an effort to find out what I like best, and working with photo-editing software to create the type of imagery I feel compelled to use in my art quilting.

Under the Boardwalk
27" × 17"
(69 × 43 cm)

materials

Bubble Jet Set 2000	Photo-editing software such as Adobe Photoshop or Adobe Photoshop Elements
Fabric of your choice for printing	
Plastic tub for soaking your fabric	Ink-jet printer and paper
Digital camera	Freezer paper
Computer	Iron and ironing board

notes on materials

I use an ink-jet printer that takes dye-based inks to do my digital printing. To make the ink permanent, the fabric must be pretreated with a fixative. I use Bubble Jet Set 2000 because it does not affect the hand of the fabric in any way.

Bubble Jet Set allows you to print on whatever fabrics you choose—you aren't limited to commercially prepared sheets or rolls of fabric available for digital printing. I have successfully printed digital images on muslin, silk habotai, silk organza, silk gauze, linen, heavy cotton and rayon, osna-burg homespun cotton, cotton flannel, and raw silk. I recommend either Photoshop or Photoshop Elements for photo-editing software. Any version of Photoshop will work, from the current Creative Suite editions back through Photoshop 6 or 7. Finally, you will need a digital camera. It need not be fancy; my Canon PowerShot is several years old and works just fine.

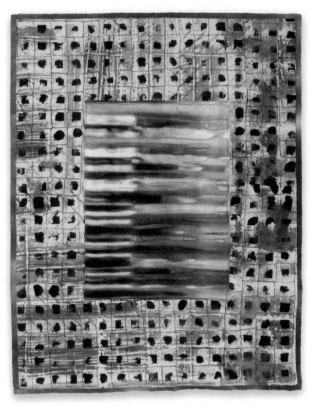

Reflection Squared 19½" × 15" (49.5 × 38 cm)

My primary interest in digital imagery lies not in reproducing or manipulating typical photographs but in looking for overall texture and pattern possibilities within an image, as well as how texture, pattern, shape, line, and color can be drawn out and perhaps exaggerated through digital manipulation.

After my digital images are printed on fabric, I use them as either a focal point in a quilt or as a design element. The printed fabric loses the mystique of being a digital image and becomes another piece of handmade fabric. The only difference is that the surface design occurred with an ink-jet printer, instead of a printing plate, a deconstructed silk screen, or any other technique. When creating my art quilts, I combine these digital fabrics with other surface-designed fabrics.

Directions

1   Tear your fabric into 8½" × 11" (21.5 × 28 cm) pieces. (You can also cut it, but I find that fringed edges add wonderful texture to a piece.) Place your fabric in a plastic tub, saturate it with Bubble Jet Set, and let it sit for about fifteen minutes. Wring it out and allow it to air-dry. Pour the used Bubble Jet Set back into the bottle to reuse later on.

2   Grab your camera and go out for a walk. As you're scanning the environment for possible subjects for digital manipulation, keep in mind key design elements—pattern, texture, shape, line, and color—and photograph whatever you see that has future fabric design potential (see Find Digital Imagery, opposite).

3   Transfer the photos to your computer and store them in a new folder so they're all accessible in one place.

4   Open one of your photos in your photo-editing software. You may want to crop the image to get a close-up of an interesting area. The first manipulation will most likely be adjusting the brightness and contrast (in Photoshop Elements 7, this is under the Enhance tab, in Adjust Lighting). Often, digital images raw from the camera need to have the brightness reduced and the contrast boosted. Make these adjustments to your liking and then save the image. This is now your original image; from here you can make further adjustments, but you'll have this version to come back to later if you want to do something different.

5   Adjust the hue and saturation of the image (in Photoshop Elements 7, this is under the Enhance tab, in Adjust Color), playing around with the intensity of the colors in the photo. If you get something you like, save the image with a new file name. For example, if the original image is IMG_123, save this new image as IMG_123A.

6   If you like, you can completely change the colors of the image by moving the hue slider. Either save this adjustment as another image, designating it B, or save it over the A image. Typically, I do all my manipulations

on one version of the image and save that as my A image since I can always go back to the saved original and start over.

7 Now mess around with filters and have fun. You can preview any filter on your image before selecting it; you can combine filters, soften or harden the image, stylize it, add texture, or distort or polarize. In short, you can completely change the way an image looks.

8 Print out different versions of your image onto paper until you find one that you would like to have on your fabric.

9 Iron one of your rectangles of pretreated fabric to the shiny side of an 8½" × 11" (21.5 × 28 cm) piece of freezer paper. I always use one layer of freezer paper under the fabric unless I am working with raw silk, in which case I use two sheets of paper, one on top of the other.

10 Print out the fabric, remove the freezer paper, and iron your fabric to set the image.

Now you have a piece of digitally printed fabric entirely of your own design. Incorporate it into a planned quilt or build a quilt around the digital image. There are no limits to what you can do with digital imagery. ■

find digital imagery

Texture and pattern are everywhere; just take a look around. Clusters of palm fronds, corrugated metal siding, tree bark, rows of mailboxes or telephone poles, pebbles and rocks, reflections in glass, rolls of paper, peeling paint, wood walls—there's no shortage of interesting imagery to manipulate. One of my favorite digital subjects is my own surface-designed fabric. Every time I create new fabric, I always photograph the best pieces.

While having a photographic record of your work is a good idea in and of itself, a less obvious benefit is that if you've created a really wonderful piece of fabric, having a digital image of it means you can work with the design indefinitely and in nearly limitless ways. And don't forget to go through photos you may already have on your computer; some may hold interesting possibilities for manipulation.

Experiments with Thermofax Printing

Easy Methods for Unconventional Surface Design

Lynn Krawczyk

MY OBSESSION with screen printing revolves around the humble Thermofax screen. These silk screens are created using a Thermofax machine, an old photocopy technology. They are incredibly easy to use and play well with a variety of printing mediums.

Depending on the medium, I use either a sponge brush, paintbrush, or plastic scraper to print my image. I use different techniques with different mediums in order to achieve a variety of effects. Try out some of these variations—you'll be a screen-printing maniac in no time flat!

Perched
10" × 10"
(25.5 × 25.5 cm)

Process photos
by Jacqueline Lams

materials

Thermofax screens (Purchase prepared screens or create your own with a Thermofax machine.)	Paintbrush
	Squeegee or plastic spackle tool
Prepared for Dyeing (PFD) fabric	Screen-printing paints
Sponge brush	Protective gloves

PRINTING WITH PAINT

I classify printing with paint into two categories: solid printing and scuff printing. Solid printing creates a complete bold print of the image, while scuff printing produces ghostlike images that are ideal for creating layers or backgrounds.

SOLID PRINTING

1 Cut about 1" (2.5 cm) off the end of a sponge brush to make it more stable. Lay the Thermofax screen with smooth side down on your fabric. Hold the screen in place by pressing down along the duct-taped edge on the top of the screen.

2 Squirt paint onto the screen and brush the paint across the image on the screen with the sponge brush (**Figure 1**).

3 Pull back the screen to reveal the image (**Figure 2**).

SCUFF PRINTING

This kind of printing produces partial, light images that add depth to your fabric. The steps are the same as for solid printing, except you squirt only a small amount of paint onto the screen, then brush lightly across individual areas rather than the entire image (**Figures 3 and 4**).

REPEAT PRINTING

Repeat printing refers to creating a repeated pattern of the same image, but it doesn't have to look uninspired. With the following approach, it's possible to produce prints that don't have specks of unwanted paint without having to wait for the paint to dry in between prints.

1 Start by printing an image in the center of the fabric, following the basic procedure for solid printing.

2 Lay the screen down for the next print, overlapping the screen onto the edges of wet paint from the previous print. As long as you don't reposition the screen, the paint won't smudge. Be sure to hold the screen in place along an edge that is not lying across the wet paint (**Figure 5**).

3 Print your image and pull back the screen. Before you create another print, check the edges of the duct tape and the back of the screen for any paint spots. If there are spots, place the screen, paint side down, on a dry paper towel and wipe off the unwanted paint.

4 Repeat Steps 2 and 3 until you've covered the entire piece of fabric, working from the inside and out toward the edges. Print the image at different angles to create movement in the print and print off the edges of the fabric to create a more organic design **(Figure 6)**.

- -

Tip: If you're doing a repeat print over a large piece of fabric, you may have to pause partway through and wash your screen to prevent dried paint from clogging the screen.

- -

Working with Thermofax Screens

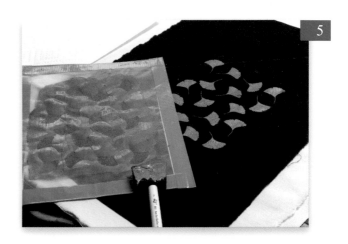

- **Store** Thermofax screens flat; a crease can form if they are folded.

- **If** you have commercial fabrics that you are no longer fond of, try printing on them to create new designs.

- **Be** sure to heat-set your prints before laundering them.

- **Use** paint that is formulated for screen printing. It stays wet longer, and regular acrylic craft paint will damage your screen.

- **Never** let paint or other mediums dry on your screen. Wash screens with plain tepid water and a soft sponge. Avoid scrubbing; a gentle washing will make the screen last longer. Blot screens dry with paper towels or allow them to air-dry before printing with them again. Never soak your screens in water. ■

THE EFFECTIVE ARTIST STATEMENT

Jane Dávila

WRITING AN ARTIST STATEMENT is a useful exercise. Taking the time to express why you make your art can help clarify your artistic goals and direction.

Your artist statement will be a key part of your presentation to any exhibition or gallery that shows your work. Your statement can be about a whole body of work, a series, or one particular piece. Most artists write their statement in the first person (as if you were talking to someone). An artist statement represents you and gives the viewer some insight into you and your art.

You can also send out your statement with press releases, letters of interest, and to collectors. An artist statement is not a biography, a CV, or a list of accomplishments and awards. It should be easy to understand and not irritating, pretentious, or cute.

The ideal artist statement is succinct and easy to read and understand. It can be as short as a few sentences and should not be longer than one page. In general, the typical artist statement is three paragraphs with three to five sentences in each.

The process of writing your statement will help you to think deeply about your process, your goals, and the work itself. Drawing out and examining your motivations will help you evaluate your progress as an artist and to speak confidently and clearly about your work.

Getting Started

Here are some steps that will assist you in writing your statement.

1 Write down words to describe your art. For example: colorful, powerful, joyous, morose, well-constructed, spontaneous.

2 Write down phrases to describe your processes: fabric collage, thread painting, immersion dyeing, meticulous piecing, raw-edge appliqué.

3 Make long lists; it's always better to have too many words or phrases than not enough. You can pare down as necessary. Try linking some of the words and phrases into sentences.

ASK YOURSELF THESE QUESTIONS

• Why do you make art?

• How do you make your art?

• What materials do you use?

• What does your art mean to you?

Art by Jane Dávila

- Are you trying to convey any emotions?

- What inspires you?

- Are there major influences in your work?

- How do your technique, style, and methods relate to your medium?

Use the answers to these questions to flesh out a typical three-paragraph statement. In paragraph one, talk about why you make the art that you do. What influences you and inspires you? In the second paragraph, explain a little about your processes and the materials you use. And in the final paragraph, you can address your current work or a specific piece of work,

explaining in more detail how and why you made it. Leave room for the viewer to see things for themselves in your work; don't dictate what they should see or feel.

After you have written a rough draft, have at least one other person read it. You want to make sure it sounds authentic and that it doesn't have typos or grammatical errors.

Create an overall artist statement and then adapt it for specific purposes. An artist statement should change as you change and as your work changes. It is not a static document but a living one. The very first statement is the hardest to write; it all gets easier from there. ∎

People, Pets, and More
representation
in art quilting

FABRIC PORTRAITS—whether they feature the human or animal form—are some of the most celebrated art quilts today. There are numerous ways to construct portrait-style quilts, but quilters often tell me that they are apprehensive about their abilities to represent the human form in fabric, especially when it comes to making a realistic-looking face. Bonnie McCaffery, demystifies the process. You'll also find ideas here for adding figures and beloved pets to your quilts, and for using text to add another element to representational quilts. Finally, two great articles will help you with thread sketching and thread painting with realistic results.

Leni Levenson Wiener, *Twilight Time* 19" × 22" (48.5 × 56 cm)

Making Faces

Bonnie McCaffery

Contemplation III: Oh Just to Be
44" × 50"
(112 × 127 cm)

WHAT IS IT ABOUT A FACE that draws us in and makes us want to take a closer look? Quilters who want to incorporate a human element into their quilts may be daunted by the notion of drawing or painting a human face. Yet anyone can do it with the help of a few simple tricks. There is no need to be a portrait artist; instead, a photograph, a transparency sheet, and a permanent fine-point marker will start you on your way to creating painted fabric faces.

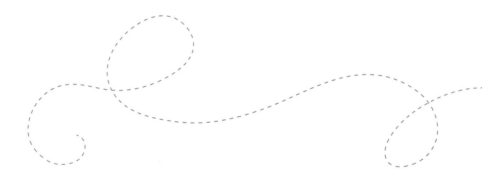

materials

A photograph of your subject	Cup for water
An acetate sheet or clear report cover	Paint palette or white plastic-coated paper plate
Permanent black fine-point marker	Plain white paper towels
Fabric to match skin color	Spray bottle with water
Good-quality paintbrushes: round size 3–5, liner size 0, scrubber brush size 3	DecoArt SoSoft acrylic fabric paint

Original photograph (left) and photograph with transparency on top for marking key features.

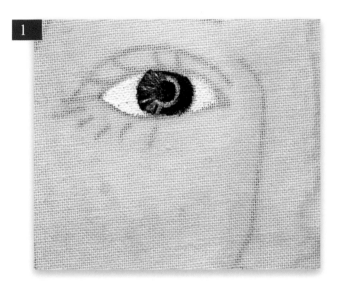

Photography

The first thing you will need is a photograph of a face. I recommend taking your own photo rather than using a professional photo to avoid copyright issues. Be sure that the photo isn't fuzzy or blurry and that the details of the face are clearly visible. Once you have a good photo, enlarge it to be whatever size you would like the face to be; 6" × 7" (15 × 18 cm) is a good finished size to try this painting process for the first time. Enlarge your photo with a scanner or take it to a copy center.

Guideline Drawing

The next step is to create a guideline drawing—this is the key to placing facial features in the correct location. Place your enlarged color copy under a sheet of acetate or inside a clear report cover. Using a permanent black fine-point marker, trace onto the acetate the outline of the face, lips, eyes, and eyebrows, as well as any noticeable lines on the nose. Shadow and highlight areas can also be indicated. Mark the top of the head and any area underneath hair by approximating the shape of the skull. Guidelines for the eyes should include the iris, pupil, a few lashes, and the crease in the eyelid **(Figure 1)**.

Painting

You are now ready to start painting. Gather all of your supplies together, along with your pre-washed and pressed fabric.

Slide a white piece of paper underneath your acetate or inside the report cover. Place your enlarged color copy nearby for reference. Tape the fabric to the guideline drawing to prevent it from slipping as you work. Using a pencil, lightly draw a few reference points such as the top of the head and the base of the neck.

SHADING

Dampen the fabric with a spray bottle to help the paint flow. Squeeze a drop of burnt sienna paint onto the palette. Mix in water

dry brush technique

Load the scrubber brush as you would when stenciling (cover the tips of the bristles in paint by dabbing the brush at a 90-degree angle into the paint). Remove most of the paint by rubbing the brush on a paper towel. Think of it as a dirty brush with just a touch of color on it.

Autumn 28" × 35" (71 × 89 cm)

using the round paintbrush, diluting the paint quite a bit. Test the darkness of the paint in an area away from the face to make sure the color is correct. Referring to your photograph and the guidelines, begin to add shadows to the face, starting in the darkest areas and gradually progressing until you are satisfied with the shading. The paint will lighten a bit when it is dry.

Carefully lift the fabric from the acetate. Place the fabric, paint side down, between two white paper towels and iron until dry. From this point on, do not add water to the paint, as it will encourage the paint to flow.

Wipe the acetate sheet with a dry paper towel, removing any excess paint. Re-tape the painted face over the guideline drawing, using the drawn reference points to align the image.

LIPS Select a paint color that closely matches the color in the photograph. Fill in the lips with a base coat using the round brush. While the paint is still wet, pick up a little burnt sienna and add some shading in the space between the two lips and anywhere else that the lips look darker. Use the brush to blend the colors. To add highlights, use peach or white. Stroke in the highlights and then blend.

NOSE The nostrils are painted with burnt sienna and the round brush. Use a very light hand with very little paint. Add shadows around the nose using the dry brush shading technique, first testing on an unused area of the fabric.

Daydream Believer 16" × 22" (40.5 × 56 cm)

Tips

- Paint what you see in the photograph, not what you know.

- Wet-on-wet shading errors can sometimes be remedied by immediately rinsing the brush out, loading it with clean water, and brushing clean water to the area just painted. Then use a clean paper towel to lift out some of the color.

photography tips

Take your photograph outdoors in the shade on a bright day.

Stand close to the subject to get good facial details.

Have your subject smile or have a pleasant expression without showing their teeth.

You can use a digital photo—just enlarge to the desired size and print in color. You can even create your guideline drawing in a photo-editing program and then just print the guideline drawing.

Refer to the photograph and the guideline drawing for the proper location of shadows. Be sure to use very small strokes; errors in shading cannot be easily fixed.

EYES While you still have the scrubber brush loaded with paint, add some more shading to the eye area. If it is difficult to see your guideline drawing through the fabric, you can transfer the lines to the fabric by tracing lightly with a pencil.

Paint the white area around the iris using the round brush. Sometimes there is shading on the whites of the eyes; look carefully at your photograph. It may be light blue/gray or possibly yellow/brown. Mix a little of the color with white and add these shadows.

Clean the brush and paint the pupil with black paint. Paint a ring of black paint around the iris. While the paint is still wet, paint a ring of eye color inside the black ring. Pick up a tiny bit of white on the tip of the brush. Stroke in radiating lines around the pupil from the outer black ring inward. This will blend the colors, creating a multicolored look of the iris. Pick up more white as needed. Finally, repaint the pupil of the eye with black paint.

EYELIDS The liner brush is used for very fine lines. It is important to use fresh paint and not paint that has been sitting on the palette. You may also want to use a tiny bit of DecoArt Brush & Blend Extender mixed with the paint to help it flow more smoothly without watering it down. Use the fine liner brush and burnt sienna paint to add the crease in the eyelid. There may also be defining lines immediately above and below the eye.

EYELASHES AND EYEBROWS Determine the color for the eyelashes. It might be black, brown, or a mixture of the two. Carefully examine your photograph to see in which direction the eyelashes curve. They may change direction as they move across the eyelid. Reload the paintbrush often. You may only be able to paint two or three eyelashes at a time.

The eyebrows are painted in a similar fashion to the eyelashes. Determine the appropriate color, note the direction in which the eyebrows grow, and paint only a few hairs at a time.

One of the tricks of portrait artists is to add a small highlight to the eye, making it come to life. Pick up a tiny bit of white paint on the point of a clean round brush. Just touch it to the eye to add a highlight. It should be in the same location in each eye.

Let the painted face dry completely.

Finishing Touches

You are now ready to appliqué the face to your background, add hair and clothing, and finish your quilt.

One method of adding hair is to create "fantasy fabric" by capturing a variety of embellishments under a sheer layer of tulle and stitching with invisible thread. Place a piece of tear-away stabilizer under the background fabric before creating your fantasy fabric. Stitch with invisible thread using a size 80 sewing machine needle, placing stitches close enough together to hold the cut fabrics and other items in place under the tulle. Only stitch where there is hair; do not stitch on the face itself. Remove the stabilizer.

You've done it! I hope you are now inspired to experiment further and create a family portrait. ■

Creating
Figures in Fabric

Leni Levenson Wiener

MANY ART QUILTERS ARE INTIMIDATED by figures and objects that seem complex or complicated and may not attempt to include them in their work. The trick is in knowing how to break these figures down into manageable pieces so that they are not so overwhelming.

Sand Gets Everywhere
18" × 17"
(45.5 × 43 cm)

materials

Photo of your choice	Toothpicks
Computer and printer, or a copy machine, for enlarging photo	Fabric glue
	Fabrics for quilt top
Fabrics in a range of values that correspond with photo	Fabric for quilt back
Red viewer, such as a Ruby Beholder	Thin batting
Tracing paper	Sewing machine with a darning foot
Freezer paper	Monofilament thread
Iron	White thread

My art quilts begin with a photo, which frees me from worrying about proportion, perspective, and the placement of shadows; all the information I need is already there for me. The key to translating photos into fabric lies in determining values in order to choose the right fabrics. Value is the relative light/medium/dark of all the colors in each section. Breaking down complex figures based on value, and then working on one portion of the design at a time, is my method for success.

Directions

1 When you have selected the photo that you would like to translate into a quilt, make a working pattern from this photo. Using a computer and printer, or a commercial copy machine, blow up the primary components of your photo to the size they will be in the final art quilt **(Figure 1)**. This pattern can be black and white, as your fabrics will be chosen by value, not color.

- -

Tip: If you are comfortable using Adobe Photoshop or Adobe Photoshop Elements, you can use the Cutout filter to simplify the photo before enlarging it, but this is not essential.

- -

2 Make a very rough tracing of the main figure in your pattern onto tracing paper. This tracing will become the template for the placement of elements as they are completed; it does not need details, just the main components of the figure to insure their proper placement when they are put together. For *Brown Bag Lunch*, I began with a template of the sitting man **(Figure 2)**.

3 Select one section of this main figure and start assigning values to the different colors within it. Looking at the photo through a red viewer (such as a Ruby Beholder) makes it easier to see values than it is with the naked eye, as the colors disappear and only their values remain. Identify the value changes on the pattern and number them from lightest to darkest. I began with the man's face and identified five values of skin tone **(Figure 3)**.

4 Select two fabrics from your stash and look at them through the viewer. (I chose beige fabrics to correspond with the man's skin.) Put the lighter one to the left and the darker one to the right. If they look the same through the viewer, eliminate one and replace it. Take a third fabric, lay it beside these two and determine where it fits in from lightest to darkest,

or eliminate it if it is the same value as something already in the group. Continue until you have selected a range of fabrics from light to dark. Select more fabrics than you will need so that you have a variety of values to choose from.

Tip: Remember that sometimes the perfect value is actually the back of one of your fabrics.

---

5 Using the red viewer again, determine the final fabrics by comparing each of the selected fabrics to a corresponding number in the pattern. Make sure that your fabric choices not only graduate from light to dark, but that they correctly relate to the values in the pattern **(Figure 4, page 86)**.

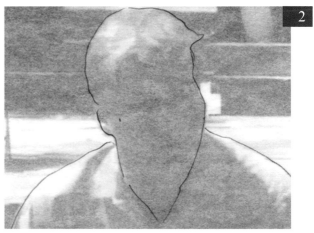

6 When you have established the fabrics, make a tracing paper template of the section you are working on; this will guide the placement of each fabric piece once it is cut **(Figure 5, page 86)**.

7 Trace the area of each numbered value in this section onto freezer paper; be sure you are writing on the paper side, not the shiny side. Use dotted lines on the freezer paper templates to indicate areas that will overlap **(Figure 6, page 86)**. You will want your fabric pieces to overlap a bit; if they butt up against each other, they may shift while you are sewing them to the background fabric and leave gaps.

Tip: A light box is very helpful for tracing; if you don't have one, a window makes a great light box during the day.

---

8 Identify which value covers the largest area; you will use the corresponding fabric as the foundation. I used the No. 3 value fabric as the foundation for the face. Make a freezer paper template for the entire section and place it onto the top of the

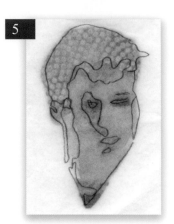

foundation fabric, shiny side down; press it gently with a warm iron so that it adheres to the fabric. Carefully cut out the shape and peel the freezer paper off the back.

9 Repeat this process for the other fabrics, pressing the traced freezer paper templates to the appropriate fabrics, cutting out the shapes, removing the paper, and placing them on the foundation fabric as you go. It is not necessary to work in numerical order.

10 When all the pieces are cut, lay the tracing paper template on top to insure their proper placement. Rearrange the fabrics as necessary until they are aligned with the template.

11 Using a toothpick, put a tiny dab of fabric glue under each cut piece. You have now finished the first element of your figure **(Figure 7)**, and all other elements are completed in this manner. There are no rules to establish what constitutes an element—just a logical and workable section of similar color. In my quilt, the shirt, the pants, the hair, and the paper bag were all treated as individual elements.

- -

Tip: Determine values and fabrics for each element as you come to it. You do not have to match the colors in the photo; as long as the values are correct, you can make decisions about colors and fabric patterns based on how they relate to each other, and how they help tell a story or set a mood.

- -

12 When all the elements of the figure are complete, position them on your background fabric, which should be constructed in the same way as the figures. Lay the full tracing paper template on top and nudge each element into place. Glue everything together with a toothpick and fabric glue, again using as little glue as possible.

13 When you are happy with the final composition, carefully press the quilt top and lay it onto thin batting. Attach the pieces with raw-edge machine appliqué: use clear monofilament thread (with white thread in the bobbin) and a darning foot to secure the edges of all the pieces using free-motion stitching. Do this before adding the backing fabric so that the finished quilt back will have a minimal amount of stitching and look clean and neat.

14 Add the backing fabric, do a small amount of functional quilting through all three layers, and finish the edges. ■

Brown Bag Lunch 12" × 15" (30.5 × 38 cm)

Pet-ty
Journal Portraits

Pokey Bolton

LET'S FACE IT: we animal owners are a little obsessed with our furry kids. We prominently display them as screen savers on our computers, harbor a library of funny photos on our smartphones, and some of us even like to upload videos of our animal children doing stupid pet tricks onto YouTube . . . and tell everyone we meet to go have a look *(cough)*.

Sophie
8" × 11"
(20.5 x 28 cm)

materials

9" × 12" (23 × 30.5 cm) backing fabric	Sewing machine with free-motion stitching capability
9" × 12" (23 × 30.5 cm) batting	Threads in various colors (I used #30 cotton thread.)
Scraps of quilt fabrics in analogous colors (Fabrics with subtle patterns and textures, such as batiks, work.)	Temporary adhesive spray such as J.T. Trading 505 Spray and Fix
Scraps of organza in colors similar to your fabric scraps	Fabric scissors
Thermofax screen or stencil of your furry subject	Newspaper or drop cloth to protect work surface
Screen-printing paint and squeegee	

What better way to celebrate our beloved animal children than by capturing them in a small journal-quilt–sized fabric collage? This fun, easy, and colorful quilt project is great for practicing your free-motion stitching and thread-sketching skills. For the central animal image, I used a Thermofax image of my pooch, but there are other options as well: you can create a stencil from a picture of your animal or make an image transfer using a black-and-white photocopy of your pet, soft gel medium, and a transparency.

Directions

1 Following the manufacturer's instructions, use the temporary spray adhesive to adhere the backing fabric to your batting.

2 Turn your batting and backing fabric over so the batting is right side up and start to arrange your torn bits of fabric scraps on the batting. Work quickly and don't over-think the placement of your scraps. This is a freeform collage process and your free-motion stitching and animal image will integrate all of the elements. When you are happy with the composition of your background, lightly tack the scraps down using the adhesive spray.

3 To create added depth and interest, cut out bits of your colored organza and place them on top of the scraps in various parts. Tack them in place with the temporary adhesive spray.

4 Take your fabric collage to your sewing machine and heavily free-motion stitch all over. Make swirls, flowers, circles, squares, doodles, write your pet's name, echo the patterns in the fabrics, etc. The point is to heavily stitch your piece in order to create movement and to permanently tack all of the scraps in place.

Tip: You do not have to stitch your collage before screen printing or stenciling, though I often do because I like getting the impression of the image on top of both thread and fabric.

5 Now comes the fun part! Protect your work surface with newspaper or a drop cloth and position your Thermofax screen or stencil of your pet on top of your collage. If you are using a screen, put a dollop of print paint all the way across the top of the screen and use your squeegee to pull the paint down toward you. Gently and carefully lift the screen from your collage.

6 Allow the paint to dry, then echo the lines of your pet with more thread painting. For *Sophie*, I chose green thread to contrast with the background. You can also completely cover up the paint lines with thread if you feel they are a little heavy.

7 Finish your small quilt with a zigzag or satin-stitch edge or a narrow binding. ∎

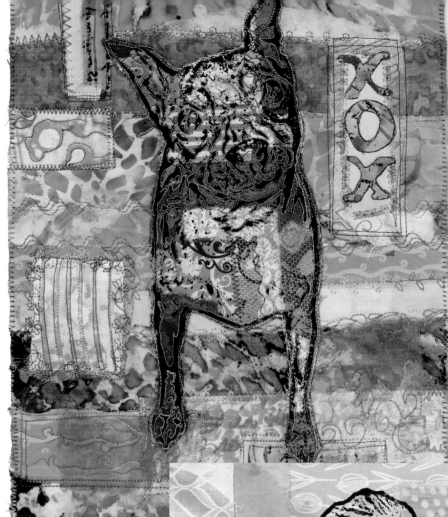

Louie, Louie
11" × 8" (28 × 20.5 cm)

Sophie on Green
8" × 11" (20.5 × 28 cm)

Text Messaging

Sticker-Resist Fabric Painting

Enid Gjelten Weichselbaum

I LOVE COLOR, fabric, music, and writing. When I create quilts, words walk through my head as I am surrounded by beautiful color and fabric. My quilts have always spoken to me; now they talk to others, too.

Sticker-resist fabric painting is a simple and quick way to achieve crisp and unique typography in your art quilts, whether as stand-alone designs or to enhance and provide a subtle point of communication within a larger quilt. This technique is a wonderful tool for bringing more life to quilts.

materials

Protected work surface

¼ yd (23 cm) light or bright-toned fabric. Use a tone-on-tone or solid fabric. Avoid bold or large prints. Fabric should be prewashed, dried, and pressed; do not use fabric softener or dryer sheets.

5½" × 7½" (14 × 19 cm) stiff double-sided fusible stabilizer such as Pellon Peltex 72F

Pencil or chalk

Iron

Opaque textile paint in colors that contrast with your fabric

A variety of paintbrushes

Scrapbooking stickers (thin and die-cut around all parts of the letter) or your own shapes cut from adhesive-backed paper

Tweezers

Thread that complements your design

Sewing machine and a denim/jeans needle

Scissors and/or a rotary cutter

Fine-tip permanent markers in colors similar to or slightly darker than your paint

Begin with a simple design and one or two colors of paint. Once you have mastered the method, try new designs, materials, and techniques.

Directions

1   Plan out your quilt by sketching a design on a piece of paper. Ensure that your design will fit your fabric and that you have the stickers for all of the necessary letters on hand (there are never enough e's). You do not need to use the same font for all the letters; be creative and let the shape of your letters communicate the feeling of your quilt.

2   Cut a piece of the double-sided fusible stabilizer slightly larger than you wish your final piece to be. For a small wall quilt project, cut the stabilizer to 5½" × 7½" (14 × 19 cm).

3   Cut two pieces of your fabric slightly larger than the stabilizer (6" × 8" [15 × 20.5 cm]).

4   Iron the fabric to each side of the stabilizer according to the manufacturer's instructions. Be sure that it is well fused.

5   Draw your design onto the fabric using a pencil or chalk. Draw a light outline around the edge of your design; this will help with planning the layout by delineating where you will trim away the fabric and stabilizer.

6   Firmly press the stickers onto the fabric. You will need a good bond to prevent the paint from seeping under the stickers. I like to run a hot iron over the fabric just before I place my stickers; I get a nice seal, but the stickers are still removable.

7   To outline the letters, apply a small amount of paint using a somewhat dry brush. Hold the brush at a 90-degree angle to the fabric and quickly dab or pounce the brush down on the stickers

and fabric. This helps to avoid pushing the paint under the stickers. Make sure your paint is not too thin or it will bleed under the stickers. Do not use dyes.

8   Once the stickers have been outlined with paint, gently brush paint over the stickers and fabric as desired. There is no need to cover the entire surface. Allow the paint to dry.

9   When the paint is dry, add additional paint or a line drawing to your piece. Allow this to dry.

10 Carefully remove the stickers using tweezers or your fingernails, taking care to avoid scratching the paint.

11 When the surface is completely dry, press with a hot iron to set the paint. You may choose to use a silicone or fiberglass ironing sheet or parchment paper to protect your iron; however, if the paint is dry, there should be no need. Do not press the piece while the stickers are still on the surface.

12 Machine quilt as desired. Your quilting stitches should enhance the design of your quilt. You will need to use a heavy needle to prevent thread breakage since you are sewing through stabilizer and fabric that has at least one coat of paint. Go ahead and sew right off the edges if you like; the quilt will be finished with satin stitching.

13 Trim the entire piece to the desired size with a rotary cutter or very sharp scissors.

14 Finish your quilt by machine satin or zigzag stitching around the perimeter. Try to completely cover the edges. Satin stitch around the piece twice if necessary. If you are using a zigzag stitch, make sure it is wide enough to cover any thread ends and enclose the edge. Allow the needle to drop outside the edge of the fabric to completely enclose the quilt sandwich.

15 If the letters and images don't pop as you wish, use a fine-tipped indelible fabric marker to draw a shadow next to them or to outline them. Imagine a light source at one corner or side of your piece and draw a narrow shadow line on the opposite side of the letters, marking the fabric paint, not the naked fabric. Be careful; your objective is to make a crisp line, not a fuzzy one, but almost all markers will bleed a bit on the fabric.

16 Use permanent marker to write your quilt's title, your name, and the date on the back of your quilt or apply your own label. ∎

Tips

- Choose text that is simple and brief. The message will pop better if it is not complicated. The paint and stitching should also speak to your message, so you will not want long and complex text.

- As you become more experienced with this process, try different fabric types, such as silk and rip-stop nylon, to achieve different effects with the paint.

- Flexible stickers work best since stiffer stickers may stand up above the fabric, allowing paint to bleed underneath them. Thin stickers are also preferable since paint can build up against the edge of thicker ones.

- Using a variety of paintbrushes will result in different textures and designs. The best images will come from highly contrasting paint and fabric; however, interesting images may include both low and high contrast.

- Removing the stickers before the paint is fully dry may result in smudged edges and sticker remnants that are difficult to remove.

- If you are dissatisfied with your results, don't throw the whole thing away! Simply tear off the top fabric and iron on a new piece. The fusible stabilizer will still be fine.

- A heavier weight thread will do a better job of covering and binding the raw edges. A lighter weight thread will require stitches that are very close together or a second pass to cover still-exposed edges and threads.

Thread Painting

From Photo to Stitched Art

Carol Watkins

*Steppin'
Out: Red
Party Shoes
8½" × 8½"
(21.5 × 21.5 cm)*

QUILTING LED ME TO MACHINE EMBROIDERY, which in turn led me to dense thread painting. Mixing threads to create depth and shadow and to tell a story captivates me. My focus is on the color of the thread, the stitch, and on the "painting" taking shape. Everything else temporarily takes a back seat. The hours fly by as I stitch, choosing colors of thread that will continue to build depth and enhance the image.

materials

Cotton broadcloth, pre-washed to remove the sizing, or Prepared for Dyeing (PFD) fabric

InkAID (white matte pre-coat)

Wide foam brush

Freezer paper

Iron

Photoshop or other photo-editing software

Printer, preferably with pigment inks

Fusible web such as WonderUnder or MistyFuse

Heavyweight interfacing

Sewing machine with free-motion capability

Thread (I use Madeira thread)

Rotary cutter and mat

optional

Dura Textiles Ink Jet Canvas, matte finish (in place of the cotton broadcloth and inkAID)

Foam-core board, for mounting the piece

Steppin' Out: Mary Janes 8¼" × 8¼" (21 × 21 cm)

Quilting and photography emerged as passions for me at about the same time, and I thought I would have to choose between them. In a eureka moment, I realized I could combine the two, and I now use my own photos to print my fabric for quilts and thread paintings.

I start with a photo (or several), manipulate it, print it, and then stitch. The process of composing the image for use in a quilt is very important. I take my time choosing images, cropping, combining photos, removing elements of the background, enhancing color, applying filters, or performing other manipulations with my photo-editing software. By the time it is printed, the photo I use may bear little resemblance to the original.

I find inspiration everywhere, even in such diverse subjects as windows and wildflowers or shoes and boots. I am also drawn to old, rusty farm equipment, twisted metal, graffiti, and much more.

Directions

1 Choose a photograph, or several, and use your photo-editing software to digitally manipulate the image(s). First, open a photo or scan an image. Make a copy of it and close the original. You can do various manipulations on the copy of your photo. I suggest starting with fairly simple designs or shapes.

2 Prime your cotton broadcloth with inkAID. The inkAID will hold the ink from the printer on the surface of the fabric for a crisp, sharp, detailed image. It also stiffens the fabric, which lessens distortion that would otherwise result with heavy stitching.

3 Cut the cotton about 1" (2.5 cm) larger than the final print and iron the back side of the fabric to the shiny side of an 8½" × 11" (21.5 × 28 cm) piece of freezer paper. I have made the mistake of ironing the inkAID side of the prepared fabric to the freezer paper, so watch out for this. Trim with a sharp rotary cutter and iron again.

- -

Tip: Ensuring a tight bond between the fabric and freezer paper is important for the smooth operation of the printer. If not held firmly, the ink cartridge carriage can yank the fabric. This usually stops the printer.

- -

4 Set the printer to thicker media or envelope and print using the Matte setting. While pigment inks are preferable to dye inks, either may be used. Dye inks may fade.

5 Remove the freezer-paper backing and bond the printed image to the heavy interfacing using fusible web. The interfacing helps to prevent the fabric from distorting with so much stitching.

6 Wind several bobbins with a neutral-colored thread so you will not have to interrupt your rhythm later, then lower the feed dogs, set your stitch length to 0, and attach a free-motion or darning foot.

7 Turn under the edges of your piece about ¼" (6 mm) and stitch over them, unless you are planning to add fabric borders later.

8 Print a copy of your image so you can see the details that may be obscured as you cover the image with thread. Do some stitching all over the surface and then go back, building up additional layers of color. Usually I begin "painting" smaller details before filling in large areas. Iron the piece occasionally to keep the work flat.

- -

Tip: I prefer a narrow zigzag stitch, closely spaced at a 45-degree angle. I like the way this gives a sketched line effect. But you could use a straight stitch or zigzag directly up and down. Practice various options before beginning.

- -

Your thread painting can cover the surface completely and densely so that no background shows, or you can create a sketch-like effect with heavier stitching in some areas and lighter stitching in others.

To frame your finished stitchery, cut a piece of foam core slightly smaller than the work. Handsew the piece to the foam core from the center out. The tiny stitches will be invisible. Bond the foam core to a canvas-covered stretcher. While I often finish thread paintings this way, you can also use them as details within quilts, inserts in jackets, incorporated into handbags, or whatever your imagination conjures up. These small works deserve a beautiful presentation. ■

stitching tips

- I use a Bernina sewing machine and run the bobbin thread through the eye in the finger of the bobbin case as recommended for buttonhole stitching (I work on a 1975 Bernina 830). Since this process is entirely free motion, an embroidery machine is not useful.

- I reduce the upper tension very slightly. This keeps the bobbin thread from showing on the surface so I do not need to change bobbin thread colors as I work.

- Test your stitching on a scrap sample before starting on the printed image.

- Posture and relaxation are important when doing such intense work. Relax your shoulders, breathe freely, and have your arms and wrists in optimum position. Stop and roll your shoulders regularly or get up and move around for a few minutes.

thread tips

- Rayon thread has a beautiful sheen, but cotton and poly-cotton threads are fine, too. I mix threads if I need a particular tone and do not have it in rayon. Sometimes I contrast a reflective rayon area with a flatter, less reflective area.

- I don't use multicolor thread because I want to be in control of light and dark tonal areas. I create blending by stitching and then going back into an area with more threads, overlaying lighter or darker tones or contrasting color.

Thread Sketching on Stabilizer

Karen Fricke

IT WAS ONE OF THOSE "thump myself on the head" kind of moments. I was brainstorming ways to include a photographic image in a quilt, but I wanted to try something different from just printing the photograph directly onto my fabric. I was looking for a technique that would allow more of the artist's hand to be seen, more of a representational sketch than a photograph.

I began by using a light box to trace the important features of the photo onto tear-away stabilizer. Then I pinned the stabilizer to the fabric, wrong sides together, and free-motion stitched along the traced lines from the back.

*Coqui Up
Close*
10½" × 13"
(26.5 × 33 cm)

materials

Good-quality #50 black thread
(I use Mettler and Gutterman)

Sewing machine with
free-motion capability

90/12 machine embroidery needle

Background fabric: 100 percent
cotton in a light-to-medium shade
(preferably a solid or hand-dyed
piece that reads as a solid)

Heavyweight, tear-away stabilizer
such as Pellon Stitch-n-Tear.

Permanent fine-line marker, black

Fabrics for inner border (loosely
woven), outer border, and binding

Batting and backing

The resulting free-motion embroidery image on the front of the fabric wasn't what I had hoped for. That's when the "thump myself" moment occurred. Would it be possible to print the photo directly onto the stabilizer?

This technique proved to be remarkably easy and versatile. The process begins with a digital photograph printed in grayscale from my home computer printer directly onto tear-away stabilizer. The stabilizer feeds very easily through the printer. I use a fine-line permanent marker to highlight any shading or details that were lost in the printing and free-motion stitch, using black cotton thread, following the design on the stabilizer.

When I've completed the outline of the design, I fill in the shadows and contours. When the design is complete, I remove the stabilizer and turn it over to the right side of the fabric. The resulting free-motion embroidery is remarkably like a pen-and-ink sketch.

Directions

STITCHING THE IMAGE

1   Choose a digital photograph. If it is a color photo, adjust it to grayscale and size it to suit your needs. Use personal photos or look for photos that are in the public domain and are copyright-free. Print a copy of the photo on plain paper to use as a reference while you stitch.

- -

Tip: If the direction is important to the composition of the image (for example, if you want the final image to show a right hand rather than a left), flip the photographic image on the computer. The image that prints on the stabilizer will be a reverse of the original photograph.

- -

2   Press a piece of heavyweight tear-away stabilizer flat, and trim it to 8½" × 11" (21.5 × 28 cm). Print the grayscale photo directly onto the stabilizer, with the printer

set to best printing quality. Feed each piece of stabilizer through the printer individually. Let the printer ink dry completely, preferably twenty-four hours, and then heat-set it with a dry iron.

3   Use the permanent pen to define any lost details or lines that you want to emphasize in your stitching. Hold the stabilizer image up to a piece of your fabric to make sure all essential elements are visible. Pin the stabilizer to the fabric, wrong sides together.

- -

Tip: For greater stability, use two layers of the tear-away stabilizer, with the printed sheet on top.

- -

4   Use a good quality #50 black thread in the needle and bobbin, a 90/12 embroidery needle, and a darning or free-motion foot with the feed dog down.

- -

Tip: Prepare a test sample using the same materials as your actual piece. Test the thread tension by making loops and swirls, as they show any tension problems more readily than stitching straight lines. The goal is to have even tension on the top and bottom, so that the bobbin thread is not pulled through to the top, nor is the top thread pulled through to the bottom. When you feel comfortable with the process, try other types of threads in the bobbin—a fine rayon thread gives you a very precise stitching line to achieve greater detail, perfect for a small, intricate portrait. A heavier thread, such as a #30 quilting cotton, will create a heavy line, which is ideal for a larger sketch. When you are happy with the tension, you're ready to sketch.

- -

5   Begin by stitching the outline of the image, then fill in the shadows and contours of the design, using a smooth back-and-forth motion. The most difficult part about thread sketching is to stop thinking about what you're doing, breathe, and just stitch. I stitch over each line at least twice, so that the final result mimics a pen-and-ink sketch.

6 Carefully remove the stabilizer, where possible, using a seam ripper and tweezers. Leave it in place under heavily stitched areas. Press flat.

INNER AND OUTER BORDERS

1 Tear 1¼" (3.2 cm) wide strips of a loosely woven fabric; I used Burmese cross-dyed cotton, but fine linen works nicely, too.

2 Fold the strips lengthwise, not quite in half. With the narrower width on top and the folded edge even with the raw edge of the quilt top, pin or baste the strips to the sides, trimming to fit.

3 Pin or baste the remaining lengths onto the top and bottom. The corners of this inner border will overlap.

4 Trim a strip of your outer border fabric to the length of each side; attach using ¼" (6 mm) seams and press toward the outer borders. Do the same with the top and bottom outer borders.

5 To create the fringe on the inner border, gently ease out individual threads along the raw edges.

FINISHING

1 Layer your quilt top with the batting and backing; baste. For quilting, I used a #30 variegated cotton thread and nudged the narrow border aside to free-motion stitch tiny loops and swirls.

2 In the outer border, I stitched random rectangles —the visual opposite of the loopy interior—and finished the quilt with a narrow pieced binding.

The result is a thread sketch that looks very much like a pen-and-ink drawing. You'll find that this technique is quite versatile, combining the representational attributes of a photograph with the appeal of an artist's individual rendering. ■

Print a grayscale photo directly onto tear-away stabilizer.

Use a permanent pen to define any lost details or lines.

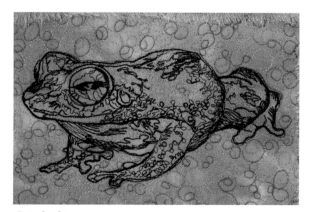

Stitched image.

MOUNT A GROUP EXHIBITION

Jane Dávila

IF YOU BELONG TO AN ART GROUP, consider mounting an exhibition to show your collective work to the public. It's a great way to get feedback about your work, generate interest in your medium, and even make some sales. An exhibition is also an excellent excuse to create new work.

Select a Venue

First, scout out some places to hold your exhibition. Office buildings, public buildings such as town halls and recreation centers, and commercial spaces such as banks and restaurants may have gallery space available. Many public libraries have gallery space. Have two or three members view the spaces once you've narrowed the choices down to a handful. Take measurements and photos to compare spaces and share the choices with your group. Ask the contact person at the venue questions, including whether they take a commission on sales, how sales are handled, who is in charge of publicity and press, insurance and other liability issues, and more.

Work Out the Details

After choosing a venue, move on to the details of the exhibition itself. Determine whether or not your exhibit will have a theme, the title for the show, the maximum and minimum sizes of work, whether there will be conformity of hanging or mounting (i.e., all work framed, all work mounted on stretched canvas, etc.), medium or media allowed in the show, and jobs for exhibiting members.

MAKE DISPLAY DECISIONS You may need to limit the number of pieces each member can present. Decide whether you will hang the work salon style (one above the other in rows with little space between works) or gallery style (one long single row with more space in between).

ASSIGN JOBS Divide jobs among the group members. You'll need a publicity person to write and distribute press releases and act as the contact person for interested press. A separate person might be responsible for Internet publicity. One person should be a liaison with the show venue, to learn things such as when the previous show will be coming down, when your show will need to come down, what refreshments are allowed, and other questions. A refreshment committee can provide snacks, appetizers, drinks, and flowers. You'll need clean-up at the end of the opening reception. If someone in your group is a graphic designer, have them create an exhibition postcard and posters. Other tasks include hanging the show; for most local shows, two to three people can do the hanging.

SET UP A BUDGET Collect funds from each member and appoint a treasurer. Determine a budget by including all potential expenses you'll incur: venue rental, postcard printing,

Pastiche 7 10" × 10" (25.5 × 25.5 cm)

refreshments and guest book for the opening, and advertising.

ESTABLISH A TIMELINE Create a timeline of all deadlines and milestones on the way to the exhibition and send frequent reminders to other members.

PRICE THE ARTWORK Each member can determine a price for their work (or note if it's not for sale). Have price lists printed up for distribution at the show. Hang labels for each work with artist's name, title, and price. Use small red dot stickers to mark work as it's sold.

PREPARE ARTIST STATEMENTS Gather all of the participants' artist statements in a binder; place it on a table near the guest book for visitors to look through.

Exhibiting with other artists will give all of you an appreciation for each other's work, as well as your own. The opening reception is the culmination of all of your hard work and the party is the perfect way to celebrate! ■

show hanging supply checklist

- ☐ Step stool
- ☐ Tape measure
- ☐ Nails
- ☐ Painter's tape
- ☐ Wall labels with artist names, titles, and prices
- ☐ Master list of all artwork
- ☐ Pencils
- ☐ Level
- ☐ Camera
- ☐ Hammer
- ☐ Eraser for smudges on the walls
- ☐ Paper towels
- ☐ Glass wipes (if work is framed under glass)
- ☐ Thread snips
- ☐ Lint roller
- ☐ The art!

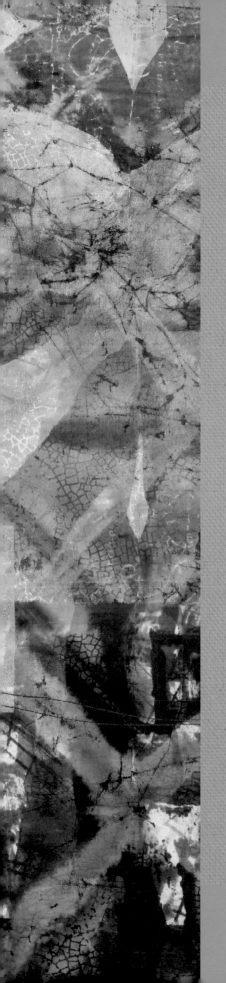

Make It Green
recycled and
natural materials

THE MOVEMENT TO GO GREEN has not been lost on fiber artists. Many quilters today use techniques and materials that are environmentally friendly as well as repurposing seemingly useless and mundane items into interesting pieces of art. After reading the ideas in this chapter, I hope you'll be inspired to recycle items such as old zipper parts or weathered scraps of steel. Here are a few additional green studio practices to consider:

- Unplug the appliances in your studio when not in use.

- Use empty egg cartons for sorting and storing beads and found objects and use plastic egg containers as palettes for fabric paint.

- Consider all of the stitching, felting, and quilting possibilities before you discard old clothing and linens.

Jane Dunnewold, *Breath*

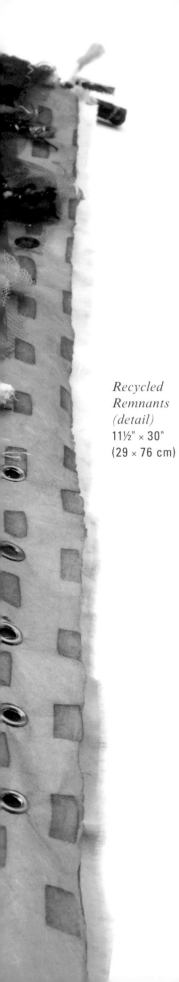

Recycled Remnants (detail)
11½" × 30"
(29 × 76 cm)

Going Green!

Recycled Wall Hangings

Belinda Spiwak

I ALWAYS HAVE A DEFINITE IDEA in my head when starting a project. The thing is, I rarely ever stay on course with that idea. The idea changes and veers until it has taken on a life of its own.

After successfully creating a square for the *Quilting Arts* Go Green! Square Quilt Challenge, I decided to make an entire wall hanging from materials that I already had on hand. I initially thought it would be a challenge to create a finished piece from my stash, but I soon realized that I had more than enough materials to create several projects.

materials

Water-soluble stabilizer, such as Sulky Solvy

Fabric scraps and strips

A variety of paper scraps (painted, collaged, stamped, embossed, dyed, handmade, and some with text)

Fiber scraps

Loose pieces of wool roving

Packaging paper or packing material

Tulle scraps in various colors

Dyed muslin or other lightweight fabric

Findings such as buttons, small metal pieces, tags, electronic parts

Favorite stamps and stamp pads

Copper paint, such as Lumiere Adirondack Color Wash

Small beads

Metallic brads

Eyelets and Crop-a-Dile tool or other eyelet setter

Glue and glue dots

Dowel or branch slightly longer than the width of your hanging

Embossed metal scraps

Sharpie extra-fine white poster paint pen

The beauty of using things that you already have is that you are giving them a new purpose. There's so much that I can do with fabric, fiber, paper, and metal scraps. Make your own unique recycled art with these simple instructions.

Directions

1 Cut a piece of water-soluble stabilizer slightly longer than the planned finished length of your wall hanging.

2 Collect fabrics, papers, fibers, wool roving, and other scraps of choice. They should be of varying lengths and widths.

3 Randomly sew the scraps onto the stabilizer in a cross-hatch pattern, where some scraps go up and down and some across. Lay smaller pieces of tulle over different areas to give a softer look (I ripped the tulle in the more open areas to give it a recycled look). I incorporated scraps of paper, fibers, roving, and packaging material as well.

- -

Tip: The scraps must overlap each other or your pattern will fall apart when the water-soluble stabilizer is removed from this layer.

- -

4 Follow the manufacturer's instructions to remove the stabilizer and then allow your piece to dry completely.

5 When your piece is dry, iron it at a medium-high setting to soften the layer. Use a dry iron with no steam. Do not hold the heat over the fiber, roving, and tulle areas too long, or they will begin to melt.

6 Brush some glue along your dowel or branch and wind some fibers down the length of it. Fold the top of your collage over the dowel or branch. Give yourself a little more room than the diameter of the dowel or branch and stitch across the width, leaving both ends open, to create a sleeve.

- -

Tip: I kept the dowel in my piece while I was completing the piece so I would not accidentally sew the openings closed.

- -

7 Find larger pieces of paper and cut out some shapes. I also cut shapes from leftover pieces of embossed metal sheeting from other projects. I used mostly diamonds and rectangles, but cut heart shapes as well. I colored some of the shapes with Adirondack Color Wash and wrote on them with the Sharpie or colored them with the copper paint. Sheet metal edges are extremely sharp; fold over the edges or sand them to minimize the risk of cutting yourself.

8 Use various found objects and put them onto the shapes for texture and contrast. I used some complementary paper and pieces of dyed muslin behind these shapes. Sew or glue them on.

9 After you have placed the findings on top of your shapes, start arranging your mixed-media scraps onto the top of this scrap layer. Pin them in place. Machine or handstitch the shapes onto the top layer. I used straight and zigzag stitching. With so much interest in the background layer, it's okay to leave some open spaces.

10 Machine or handstitch decorative elements to the bottom of this layer. I used painted paper diamonds that were cut in half and then placed so they overlapped each other; I glued small charms on top of each diamond half. I also recycled some house charms that were left over from a charm swap.

11 Add some papers to this layer for texture and interest. I used scrap paper stamped with text, tore the edges, and used walnut stain to color the edges. I also incorporated handmade paper, player piano paper, and 1" (2.5 cm) tags.

12 When you are pleased with this layer, create another layer for the backing. I took a long

piece of dyed muslin, overlapped torn pieces of yellow and green handmade paper on it, and positioned it underneath the top layer.

13 Remove the dowel or branch and using pins to keep the layers in place, sew the two layers together at the top only.

- -

Tip: I had a problem with the bottom layer shifting. I solved this problem with $3/16$" (4 mm) eyelets and a Crop-a-Dile tool. I positioned eyelets along the sides of the wall hanging so the handmade papers were adhered to the bottom muslin layer.

- -

14 Add weight to the bottom layer so that it hangs straight and doesn't curl. I started with $1/8$" (3 mm) eyelets along the bottom and used strips of dyed muslin to attach tags and small findings to the eyelets.

15 Reinsert the dowel into the sleeve of the wall hanging. I tore long strips of dyed muslin and knotted it in several places, wrapped the end of the muslin to the end of the dowel a couple of times, and tied the ends of the muslin to each end of the dowel for hanging. ■

Batik with Soy Wax

Melanie Testa

Art by Melanie Testa

A FEW YEARS AGO, a good friend looked at me and asked, "Why aren't you using soy wax?" I looked right back at her and said, "Why should I be using it?" She went on to extol the virtues of this material and stared at me like I was totally missing the boat. Well, she was right. I am now a convert, and I hope you will be, too.

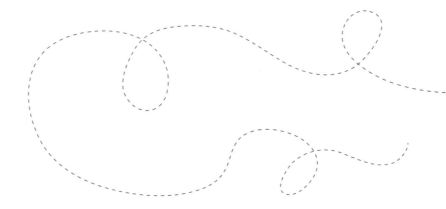

materials

Soy wax (5 lb [2.25 kilograms] is a good starting amount)	Watercolor brushes
	Newspaper
An electric pot for melting wax*	Iron
White cloth	
	optional
Mark-making tools	Sheet of Plexiglas
Textile paints (I like Jacquard Lumiere and Neopaque brands.)	Stiff squeegee
A spray bottle	Bucket
Foam brushes	*See page 115 for more on supplies.

Soy wax is a powerhouse of a resist. It is a food-grade environmentally safe alternative to paraffin. No special chemicals are required to remove it from your cloth; the wax can be removed by simply running it under hot water—its melt temperature is so low that it will not affect your plumbing. Working with soy wax takes almost all of the guesswork out of the batik process, and using soy wax with paint simplifies the technique even more.

Color

I suggest working with an analogous color range (a wedge of three neighboring colors from the color wheel). Then add a color that is opposite that wedge (for example, if you work with yellow, orange, and red, the opposite color on the color wheel will be somewhere in the blue and purple range).

White—in our case, the color of the plain cloth we're starting with—carries a great deal of weight in a design. Use white sparingly when making vivid cloth, since it creates elements that will pop within the composition. Aim for some pop, but not to the point of distraction.

Layering

Using soy wax as a resist means that you can trap previous layers of color while continuing to build and expand upon a color concept.

A good illustration of layering is the piece on page 112, which ranges from yellow to orange to red and finally to black. A potato masher was used to apply soy wax stripes along the entire length of white cloth. When the wax was dry, yellow paint was applied to the entire length. Next, a foam brush (with a small section cut from the edge) was used to stamp a wax-resist application in a meandering pattern. Next, starting about 4" (10 cm) from the top of the orange, a piece of square foam was used to resist blocks of the orange all the way down the remaining length; red was painted over this layer. Finally, starting about 5" (12.5 cm) down from the beginning of the red, a bristle brush was used to resist out large areas of the design,

creating a dry brush effect; black was then applied to this portion of the cloth.

Applying the Wax and Paint

A proper application of wax will look translucent when the fabric is held up to the light. An improper application of wax will appear opaque and sit on top of the cloth rather than sink into it.

You will be using acrylic paints in a watercolor-like fashion, creating washes of color that are layered one on top of the next. Applying these washes is pretty easy with acrylic paint; just keep your cloth fairly wet while you move the paint over its surface. The paint will remain pliable as long as the cloth is wet. Because of the wet-on-wet nature of the wash application of paint, it is necessary to have the proper translucent application of soy wax.

Create a wash over an entire area of cloth or work within or around a motif. If you do not want seepage of paint to occur, spray the cloth to a just-damp state. Continue to spritz the cloth while you work as needed. If the cloth gets too wet, the water will migrate under the wax partition; if this occurs, lift the wax and wipe away the excess water.

Directions

1 Apply your first application of wax in whatever shapes or patterns you desire.

2 Spray the entire surface of the cloth with water or simply dip the cloth into a bucket of room-temperature water.

3 Select the paint colors that you will be working with and begin by applying a wash of your lightest color **(Figure 1)**.

4 Allow the cloth to dry.

- -

Tip: Remember that you can work on many pieces of cloth at any given time; some will be drying as others are ready for their next application of wax and/or paint.

- -

5 Apply a second application of wax. Rewet the fabric, and apply a wash of medium value paint **(Figure 2)**. Continue rewetting, adding wax, and applying paint until your cloth is complete.

Tip: Most paints on the market require ironing to heat-set or bond the paint to the cloth, which will also serve to remove a predominance of the soy wax from the cloth. Keep the paint manufacturer's recommended heat setting and times in mind as you complete the next two steps.

----

6 Place your cloth between a few layers of newspaper and iron it to remove most of the soy wax. This may take several changes of newspaper and multiple applications of heat from the iron. When the majority of wax has been removed, turn the cloth wrong-side up and give it an extra dose of the iron for good measure.

7 Wash the cloth by hand using hot water and soap or simply place your samples in the washing machine for a full cycle using the hottest setting. This will remove the remainder of the wax. ■

Tip: With soy wax, you can easily create traditional batik designs such as crackles. Simply cover the entire surface of the cloth with wax, place it in a bag, and freeze it for five or ten minutes. Quickly wring the cloth before the wax warms up. This creates cracks in the wax, which you can then paint over. Use a dark color and push the paint into the cracks.

select your supplies

Supplies that you use with wax should be dedicated to wax use; do not use them for food preparation.

- ELECTRIC POT Soy wax has a melting temperature of 180°F (82.2°C) so you will need an electric pan to melt your wax. You might choose an electric skillet or a deep frying pot. Your melting pot must have a detailed temperature dial; you do not want to burn the wax by melting it at too high a temperature. Wax can be cooled, hardened, and stored for reheating in this pot.

  I use a deep-frying electric pot with sides that are 8" (20.5 cm) deep; it has a metal basket with holes to prop up tools, and its magnetic plug is easy to disengage.

- MARK-MAKING TOOLS Any tool that can withstand an extended period of time in a 180°F (82.2°C) melting pot is fair game. Many plastic items work well, as do metal objects, foam and bristle brushes, and kitchen tools.

- WORK SURFACE When using soy wax, I work on a metal workbench, which I clean with a stiff squeegee; it is easy to scrape hardened wax off this work surface and put it back into the melting pot. A piece of Plexiglas also works well.

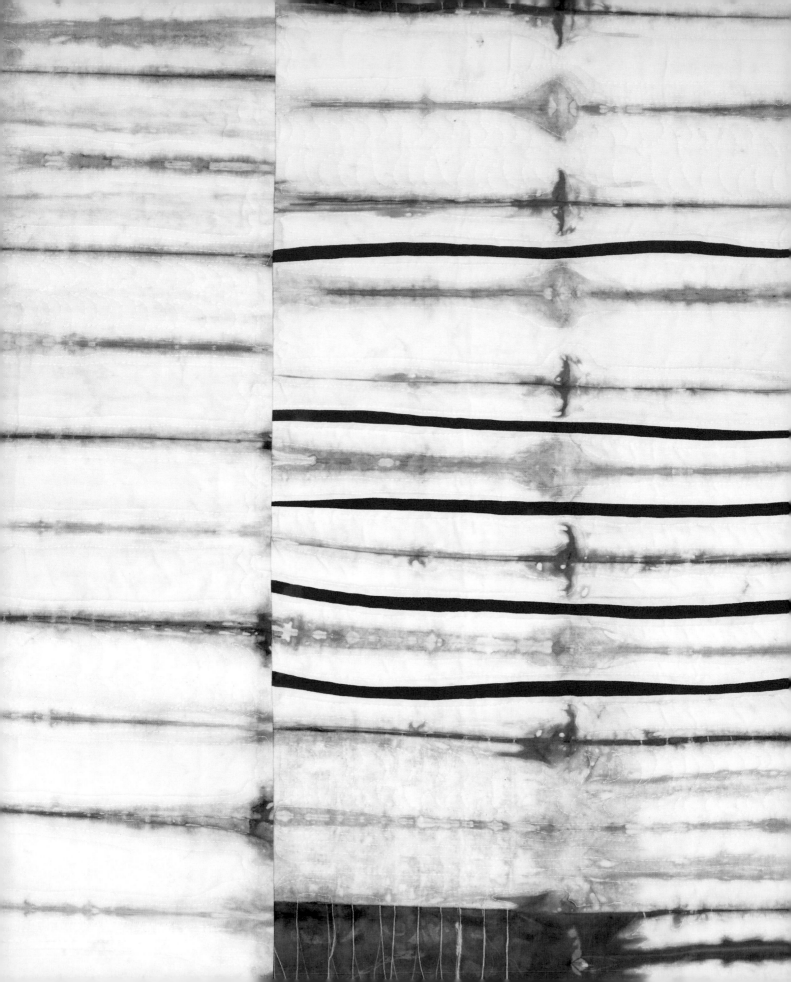

Going Green to Dye Blue

Dyeing Cottons with Indigo

Daren Pitts Redman

Red and Indigo
26" × 32"
(66 × 81.5 cm)

RECENTLY, I STARTED DYEING WITH INDIGO, a natural plant dye, because a local children's museum was having a nature display and they asked me to hold a dyeing workshop. I researched indigo's origins and resources and now have a vat continuously brewing in my studio—never pouring the contents down the drain or in the backyard.

materials

Cotton Prepared for Dyeing (PFD) fabric

Indigo powder

Lye (sodium hydroxide)

Thiourea dioxide

4-cup (237 ml) glass measuring container

Measuring spoons: 1 tablespoon (15 ml) and 1 teaspoon (5 ml)

3 plastic spoons

Paper towels

Paint stirrer (wooden)

4-gallon (15 liter) plastic bucket or a 3-gallon (11.4 liter) glass jar with lid (9" [23 cm] wide × 10" [25.5 cm] high)

Plastic dry cleaner bag(s) or other protective sheet

Plastic dishpan

Water

2-quart (1.9 liter) plastic juice jugs, recycled and clean

4 fabric swatches, 3" (7.5 cm) square, to test color

5 tea bags steeped in 2 cups (473 ml) of hot water

Synthrapol

Rubber gloves, safety glasses, and a mask or respirator

Caution: Do not use your utensils or tools for cooking or eating after you have dyed with them.

My indigo vat is a big glass three-gallon jar with a glass lid. The vat is replenished with indigo powder, lye, and thiourea dioxide between dyeing sessions.

The processes I use to "go green" when I dye with indigo include a low-water immersion technique that saves water and energy and avoids putting anything into a landfill. I use warm or cold water in the washing machine with a low water-level setting and then line dry to avoid using the dryer.

I recycle dry cleaner bags as table covers to protect the surface and repurpose household items as dyeing tools: dishpans, glass containers, and utensils. You use very small quantities of the raw ingredients, and there is no disposal of unused dye since the indigo vat is always brewing.

Indigo will dye many fabrics and is a fast and easy way to create different shades of blue for use in art quilting, collage, appliqué, book covers, etc. In my case, the indigo fabric is used in my wall hangings so I don't worry about the dye bleeding or fading after washing.

Directions

DYESTOCK FOR COTTON FABRIC

- -

Caution: You must wear rubber gloves, a mask or respirator, and safety glasses when measuring and handling lye. Handle with extreme care.

- -

1 Measure four tablespoons (59 ml) of powdered indigo into a four-cup (237 ml) glass measuring container.

2 Add ¼ cup (59 ml) of warm water (80°F [27° C]) and stir to a paste consistency. Slowly stir an additional three cups (710 ml) of warm water into the paste mixture.

3 Add two tablespoons (30 ml) of lye and stir slowly to dissolve.

4 Finally, add two tablespoons (30 ml) of thiourea dioxide and stir gently for one minute. You can take off your safety equipment now.

5 Let the indigo dye stock sit for twenty minutes. A coppery scum will form on the top. The stock should be a green-yellow or dark blue color; it is oxidizing.

6 Test the color by dipping a 3" (7.5 cm) swatch of cotton fabric into the vat. Remove it from the solution slowly and place it on a paper towel to see if it turns from green-yellow to blue when it hits the air. This oxidation process is fun to watch.

THE VAT

1 Fill two two-quart recycled juice jugs with warm water (90 to 100°F [32 to 38°C]) for a total of four quarts (3.8 liters). Pour this water into your vat and slowly add the indigo dye stock, one cup (237 ml) at a time. If the vat color is dark blue, you need to add one teaspoon (5 ml) of thiourea dioxide; it should be a clear green-yellow.

2 Stir slowly with a paint stirrer for thirty seconds. You can test a swatch of fabric again now. Remember, the vat should be a clear green-yellow. If not, add another teaspoon thiourea dioxide and stir again for thirty seconds to add oxygen back into the mixture.

- -

Tip: Place a yard (91.5 cm) of pre-dyed or undyed fabric on top of your plastic table covering to catch the drips from the fabric coming out of the vat. I use these "drip cloths" as backs and bindings for my art quilts.

- -

TYING, WRAPPING, AND DIPPING

1 Clamp, scrunch, pin, fold, pole wrap, or rubber-band the cotton PFD fabrics to create interesting patterns.

2 Using a safety pin, attach a string or piece of yarn to a corner of each of your fabrics so you can fish them out without disturbing the vat and without creating too much oxygen.

3 Put on your rubber gloves and slowly lower your fabrics into the vat; do not stir. Keep them submerged for five to ten minutes.

4 Remove the wet fabrics from the vat. Do not wring your fabrics; let them drip into the vat. After removal, lay your fabrics on another piece of fabric or on a dry-cleaner bag.

Tip: You can dip multiple times with ten to fifteen minutes between dips.

----

5 Untie or un-scrunch the fabric so the air hits the fabric surface. Let your dyed fabrics sit and oxidize overnight.

Tip: In your journal, record the number of times you dipped each piece, the minutes spent in the vat, and the minutes between dips. Some of my fabrics get dipped two times and some four; this way I get a variety of blue shades from light to dark. To get a really dark indigo blue, I dip four times for five minutes each, with fifteen minutes between each dip.

----

6 In a dishpan, with your rubber gloves on, rinse and neutralize the lye in your dyed fabrics by pouring the prepared tea over the fabrics. Swish the fabric in the tea, wring out the excess, and let it sit for one hour.

7 Wash the fabrics in the washing machine in warm water with one tablespoon (15 ml) of Synthrapol. Use two rinse and two spin cycles, or rinse until the water runs clear.

Indigo produces unique, beautiful blue hues, which is reason enough to want to use this natural dye. Going green with the process makes it all the more compelling. ■

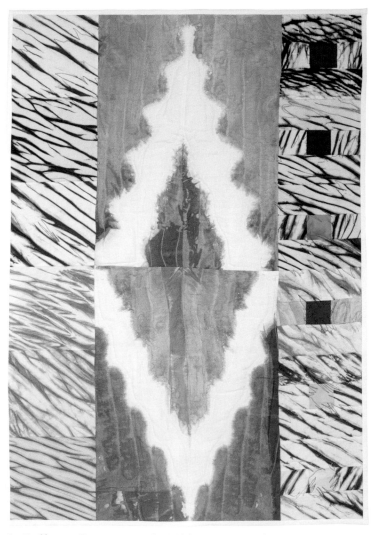

In Different Directions 41" × 29" (104 × 73.5 cm)

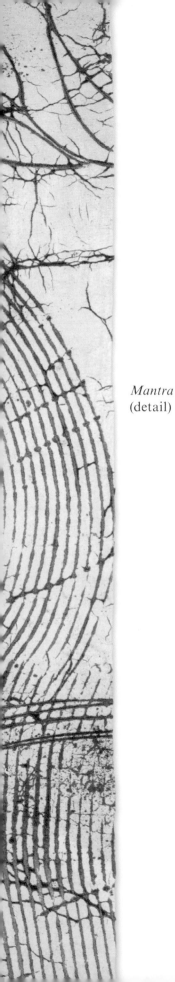

It's Irresistible!

Flour Paste Resist

Jane Dunnewold

Mantra
(detail)

I OFTEN WONDER whether artists have a special "what if" gene that other people on the planet aren't lucky enough to inherit. We all have gifts—don't get me wrong—and as a longtime teacher, I believe each of us has creative potential. But I've observed plenty of artists in exploration mode, and I can attest to the risk-taking energy generated in those studio sessions.

materials

Mixing bowl	Squeegee
Large spoon	Bristle paintbrush (wide)
Wire whisk	Wooden skewer
Measuring cup	Safety pins
White flour	Black textile paint
Cold water	Tape
Fabric in any color	Padded printing surface
T-pins	

Breakthroughs happen when you least expect them. One day, in the middle of a demonstration, I was slathering flour paste onto cloth. Thanks to a creative student, I discovered the possibilities in using flour paste as a resist and drawing into it to yield random crackle patterns combined with linear patterns, circles, and lines.

In surface-design lingo, a resist is a product or a process that temporarily blocks fabric's ability to absorb another wet medium. Flour paste is called a water-based resist because it is a temporary blocking agent. It's a resist anyone can make and use. Flour paste is nontoxic, and you probably have the ingredients you need in the kitchen cupboard right now. The paste doesn't keep overnight, so don't make more than you need for one session.

Apply the paste to any fabric. You may need to play with the application in order to get the thickness of the flour paste exactly right for the cloth you want to coat so make several samples the first time you try this. Then you can compare results once the process is complete, and the information you acquire will help you the next time around.

Apply the Flour Paste

1 Pin or tape the fabric to your padded printing surface. The fabric shrinks and curls as the paste dries, so create a taut surface before you get started. Pin the fabric securely every 1" (2.5 cm) or so along all four edges, stretching it slightly as you pin, to prevent wrinkling when the paste is applied.

2 Mix one cup (237 ml) of white flour with one cup (237 ml) of cold water. Add the water gradually. The desired consistency is roughly the equivalent of pancake batter. If the paste is too thin, add flour. If it is too thick, add cold water. Use a whisk or large spoon to stir the paste until the lumps are gone.

3 Pour flour paste across the top of the fabric sample pinned to the table. The width of the flour paste strip varies depending on the size of the sample.

4 Use the squeegee to spread the flour paste across the fabric surface and cover the entire surface. Be sure there aren't any open places you've missed.

5 If you prefer a simple crackle, allow the paste to dry thoroughly at this stage. If you want patterning, use the skewer to draw into the wet paste. Draw patterns, circles, swirls. I love to write words into the wet paste. Erase by smoothing the paste with the squeegee. When you are satisfied with the patterning, allow the paste to dry thoroughly. This could take twenty-four hours or more, depending on the humidity.

Apply the Paint

1 Remove the pins holding the fabric to the printing table. Crackle the fabric by scrunching it. The more you scrunch, the more the paint seeps into the fabric, so don't go overboard the first time.

2 Thin black textile or craft paint with water to the consistency of milk or use a thin watercolor-weight textile paint such as Setasilk or Dye-na-Flow. I suggest black paint, but any color will work. Pale colors may not show up clearly, so experiment.

3 Use a wide brush to spread the thin paint over the flour-coated surface. Work the paint into the flour paste using pressure to be sure the paint penetrates the paste. Allow the paint to dry.

After spreading flour paste on fabric with a squeegee, lines and swirls were drawn into the wet paste.

When the paste was thoroughly dry, the fabric was scrunched to crackle the surface. Thin black paint was painted over the surface and allowed to dry and set.

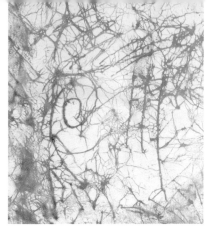

After washing out the flour paste resist, the painted fabric was ready for use.

4 Textile paint requires heat setting, but we break that rule with the flour paste resist, because you can't easily iron the flour-coated fabric, and you definitely don't want to put this fabric in the dryer. Instead, wait twenty-four hours before you wash out the fabric. The longer you wait, the more the paint sets; waiting for as long as a week will not affect the flour paste.

Wash Out the Flour Paste

1 Soak the flour-coated, painted fabric in a bucket of warm water for ten minutes. The flour paste will begin to dissolve.

2 Pour off the water and put the fabric in a washing machine on the regular cycle. Wash the fabric thoroughly. You do not need to add soap. Heavy cotton or silk noil may require two washes to remove the paste completely.

3 Dry the fabric in the dryer and press it with an iron.

After the flour paste has been removed, the fabric can be painted with textile paints, dyed and overdyed, or used exactly as it is. The potential for drawing, applying more than one color of paint to the surface, and repeated layerings of both paint and paste ensures satisfying hours of exploration. It's irresistible! ■

make your own printing surface

For the best printing results, you should lay a printing pad in between your worktable and the fabric. The quickest temporary printing surface is as simple as a blanket folded in half, smoothed and taped with masking tape to a tabletop. Make sure the blanket is smooth (no wrinkles) and don't use more than two layers of blanket—the surface will be too soft. Cover the printing surface with an old sheet to keep the felt clean.

TIME MANAGEMENT FOR ARTISTS

Jane Dávila

MANY ARTISTS THINK that the creative process operates independently of any sort of structure, that an artist works when the muse calls. In reality, most successful, productive artists got that way by being able to manage their time well—by structuring their time and by working within a schedule. Here are a few simple steps to get you started.

Account

Write down exactly how you spend your time over the course of a week or two. This will give you a really clear idea of what's eating up your time. Once you have this list you can work on what you're willing to do to change it to make more time for art. If all else fails, are you willing to get up a half hour earlier or stay up a half hour later?

Prioritize

Decide what's important to you and what you're willing to spend time doing and what you're not. What's going to change? If you make a commitment to work in your studio more hours each week, you may need to let go of other things that aren't as crucial to accomplish this.

Schedule

Scheduling specific time to create may be the single most important thing you can do to manage your time effectively. Write your studio time on your calendar and schedule other things around it.

As little as fifteen minutes in the morning and fifteen more in the afternoon adds up to three and a half hours a week. The amount of available studio time may ebb and flow from week to week, but keep it on your schedule.

Learn how to deal effectively with interruptions. Practice saying "I'm sorry, I'm working right now; I'll be done at five o'clock and I'd be happy to talk to you/help you/go with you then." You can't expect anyone else to take your schedule seriously unless you do.

Organize

Organize your supplies so you won't waste time looking for things when you could be using that time to create.

Make Lists

Make lists and sub-lists of what you'd like to accomplish. Check things off as you finish them and add new things to your list as you think of them.

Limit

Limit a task to the time it deserves. If you're working toward a deadline for something that would take a day and a half to complete but you have five days in which to do it, be careful that you don't end up using the full five days. You could be doing other things with the three and half days you technically don't need.

The structure of a schedule is meant to be liberating, not constricting. Control over your use of time will give you freedom to create and will help you accomplish more than ever. ■

Art by Jane Dávila

Embellishment and Mixed Media

too much is
never enough

I ADORE QUILTS with extreme embellishment—those quilts encrusted with beads, bits of glass, metals, buttons, small plastic toys, you name it. For example, although Frances Holliday Alford's quilts in this chapter are very small in size, they're heavy with abundant embellishment! Mary Hettsmansperger also finds beauty in everyday objects and demonstrates how they can be combined with fabrics to create eye-catching embellished quilts. Judy Coates Perez uses tea bags to make her gorgeous work. Mixed-media quilting can be a very freeing, rewarding, and fun process, and I hope this chapter inspires you to take an unconventional approach to quilting.

Frances Holliday Alford, *Analogous Split Rail in Red, Orange, and Yellow*
16" × 16" (40.5 × 40.5 cm)

Outrageous Embellishment

Frances Holliday Alford

I LOVE BEADS, BUTTONS, AND FOUND OBJECTS. If I see something glittering, I am attracted immediately. I particularly value found objects, recycled pieces, and the familiar objects of daily living. There is a drive within me that causes me to watch for objects and items, always with the idea that they will find their way into my work.

Although heavily encrusted quilts have been popular for a while, I was drawn to the idea of using objects with only their color in mind for placement. I have a system of sorting and storage that keeps all the small pieces arranged by color. I like to juxtapose common materials and luxury items in close proximity.

A Page from My Journal
9" × 11"
(23 × 28 cm)

materials

Bead soup (see page 133)

Clear glue for attaching button shanks (I use Super Glue or E-6000)

Heavy interfacing (I use Timtex)

Loosely woven fabric

Low-loft cotton batting

Embroidery floss

Silamide or other beading thread

Embroidery needle

Between or beading needle

Fray Check or clear nail polish

Bead Soup

Before starting a project, I spend some time deciding what the underlying image will be. I have done pieces that are all one color, blends of colors, and geometric forms, by using the small items from my bead soup. These items appear as a blend of color from a distance in much the same way that the Neo-Impressionists or Pointillists represented color by allowing the eye to optically mix the colors to form another color. Pointillist paintings appear to be solid colors, but when the viewer is invited in and examines the piece closer, he is able to see the sums that make the whole. I consider each sewn-down object to be my paint and that I am painting in the Pointillist method.

My bead soup consists of a variety of items. Buttons and beads are the staple, including Austrian crystals, new buttons, vintage buttons, and bulk embellishments from variety stores. I like the mix of wood, plastic, Bakelite, clay, fabric, crystal, acrylic, and resin. In addition to the buttons and beads, I am always on the lookout for old jewelry, small toys, game pieces, and plastic bottle caps. I have used small toy cars, guitar picks, refrigerator magnets, tiny blunt-nosed scissors, and plastic cards.

While sorting, I do not concern myself with value, intensity, texture, or size. I am only sorting by hue. Pale pink is in the same container with vivid scarlet and dark red. With some items, it's hard to distinguish between one color and another. If that's the case, I make a guess. For example, some maroon goes into the purple container and some lands with the red.

Two drawbacks to my method are the weight of the finished project and the cost of the materials. Because of that, I mix in some lightweight, low-cost alternatives, including paper beads, polymer clay beads, and parts of discarded credit cards and computerized hotel keys. Also, some vintage necklaces have hollow, lightweight beads that are useful in keeping the overall weight down.

Attachment Theories

I use a very heavy interfacing as a foundation. I prefer the kind that does not have any fusing material on it, as I want the needle to have as little resistance as possible. If the piece is going to be large, I will often use two layers of interfacing or make the piece in smaller components that I stitch together later.

1 Cut the foundation piece to size, add a layer of low-loft cotton batting, and then a loosely woven fabric on top. Use a loosely woven fabric so the needle can move easily through the layers. I draw lines to indicate where the colors will start and stop and usually color in enough of the surface to indicate which color is planned. Another method is to cut fabrics in the colors planned and lightly baste them in place. With this method, the underlying color can show through to enhance the final project.

2 Sew or handbaste the layers together, tucking the woven fabric under so that there will be a clean edge.

3 Attach the larger items first, using embroidery floss and a large-eyed embroidery needle. I thread a piece of floss a little longer than the length from my hand to my elbow, then double this length, thread the needle, and knot both sides at the ends. This gives me a twelve-strand thread to use for attaching beads. I like to use a variety of colors of floss and usually change colors each time I reload my needle, using a thread that is a contrasting color to the items I am attaching.

4 After the larger beads are in place, use a small between-needle and a double strand of Silamide thread to attach smaller beads and buttons. Although Silamide is my favorite, you may also use dental floss or beading thread. Do not use regular sewing thread, as it is not strong enough.

Arranging the Composition

My method for attaching items is intended to make the pieces stack up, show at angles, overlap, or stand on end.

1 Start with an item that you think needs to be showcased in some way. After it is attached, draw your needle up as close as possible to the edge of that item and add another item. Because there is no room for the pieces to spread out, they start to find room by default. I like the way a button reflects color because it is on a tilt rather that flat. It adds dimension and texture.

2 Try to make gradual shifts from larger, taller surfaces to smaller, flatter surfaces. Dramatic jumps in height and scale are not as appealing as the more subtle. I also like to group like objects to do the work that negative space might offer in a more traditional medium.

3 Decide if you want to make a large patch of bright objects or if one tiny piece might add a small glittering punctuation. I like to add a piece of another color once in a while to break up the monotony of the piece, too.

4 When making a color blend, start at one side with one of the colors and then add the other color to the other side. I mix half of each color toward the middle. It is fun to go from yellow to green or from blue to purple with tiny dabs of color arranged to allow the eye to mix the hue.

Solo Flower 21¾" × 17½" (55 × 44.5 cm)

For the piece shown above, each element—such as the flower petal and leaf also shown above—was embellished individually, then secured to the yellow background.

Finishing Touches

When the embellishment is complete, add a backing. Flatten the work from the back and determine if you first need to add another layer of interfacing for strength.

1 Choose a fabric for the back; I like to use the complementary color from the color wheel for this. Turn the edges under, making a piece the same size as the front, and attach it to the front at the edges, using a double strand of embroidery floss and a simple whipstitch. Add a hanging sleeve and a label to the back and sign and date the work.

2 Check carefully for any loose or hanging threads that need to be clipped.

3 Add Fray Check or clear nail polish to reinforce the thread on any items that look like they may not hold.

Enjoy the process, and I believe you will enjoy your completed artwork. Though you may see my influence in your completed piece, your unique style will show through.

- -

Tips

- If an item does not have a hole for sewing it to the piece, there are several methods I use to attach it.

- I can often pierce through it with a firm hand on my needle. Try sitting near a candle and put the needle into the flame and then straight into the item. Do this in a well-ventilated area with proper respect for the open flame.

- If an embellishment can't be sewn through, I often glue it to one of the button backs I purchase in bulk.

- If an item is irregular in shape, it is often possible to stitch across part of it.

- For a larger, flatter object, lay it on the fabric and sew smaller beads around it until it is protected, as a jewel would be presented in a bezel setting.

- Quality of workmanship is crucial. Poorly attached embellishments will not withstand handling.

- Use strong backing materials, such as heavy-weight interfacing or fabric. Otherwise, the weight of the embellishments will pull on the backing and it will not stay flat or hang properly.

- Do not use any item that will deteriorate or will not hold up to handling. I also avoid using anything that is offensive.

- Use double-stranded and knotted threads.

- Add to your collection of beads and other items regularly for use in future projects. It takes a lot of embellishment to cover a piece. ■

- -

A Page from My Journal, September 2005
9" × 11" (23 × 28 cm)

ingredients
for
bead soup

- *Buttons (clothing and campaign buttons)*

- *Beads*

- *Jewelry*

- *Rubber miniature toys, goldfish, Martians, etc.*

- *Small toy cars*

- *Game pieces*

- *Refrigerator magnets*

- *Industrial cast-offs such as plastic closures*

- *Small carpentry items*

- *Hair accessories, barrettes, hair ties*

- *Plastic bottle caps*

- *Shells (must be very durable)*

- *Found objects*

- *Shrink-plastic pieces*

Foiling Around

Jane Dunnewold

SHIMMER, GLIMMER, GLITZ, AND SHINE—foils add all of these, as well as textural interest, to fabrics of all kinds. Shinier than metallic fabric paint, foils are perfect as light-generating accents on clothing, quilts, or one-of-a-kind unique lengths of cloth. And foiling techniques are easy to learn and master, once you know a few simple tricks.

Foils aren't really metal at all, but a plastic surface that looks like metal and is bonded to clear cellophane; the cellophane is peeled away after the foil has been bonded to the fabric. Foils are available in a wide range of colors and patterns, including holographic and rainbow versions.

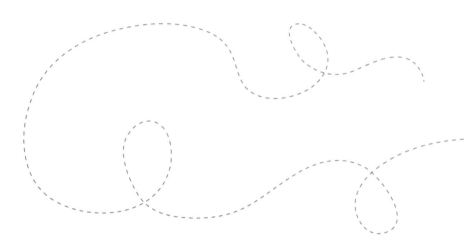

materials

Metallic foil sheets	Brushes, stamps, or stencils
Permanent fabric glue	Iron
Fabric for foiling	Hard padded surface

Adhesives

Choosing the correct adhesive is critical to successful foiling. There are several adhesives available. In general, an adhesive must meet two criteria to be appropriate for permanent foiling on fabric. First, the glue must be water-soluble. This means that while the glue is wet, water can be used to wash off both your tools and your fabric. If in doubt about your adhesive choice, read the label. If the directions say water will remove the glue while it is still wet, you have the right product.

Second, the glue must be made for fabric and permanent when dry. Water-soluble glues are like fabric paints—they can be cleaned up with water, but once dry, they are permanent. This is important as you want your foiling to stay put—especially if you are applying it to a surface you might clean often.

Fabric

The fabric you choose to foil also plays a role in your success. Very smooth fabrics such as silk charmeuse, China silk, rayon, and combed cotton are excellent choices for foiling because the smooth, even surface of the cloth will allow even foil application. If the surface is textured—such as a silk noil or a heavy rustic cotton—then the foil will be harder to apply. Fabrics should always be pre-washed before foil is applied. If you have previously dyed your fabric or printed it with fabric paints, be sure the processes have been stabilized before proceeding with foiling (stabilizing your fabric means removal of all excess dye, heat-setting paints, and whatever else it takes to be sure your cloth won't bleed, fade, or lose paint after you've added the foil).

Think of foiling as one of the final steps in your creative process. Foils will withstand some wear and tear, but they are not candidates for a dye bucket, and some paints won't stick to them when applied after the foiling has already been completed.

Applying Adhesives

Foiling adhesives are very similar to fabric paints in consistency, so they can be applied just like paint. Brush adhesive onto a stamp and then stamp it onto your fabric.

You can also apply the glue through a stencil, using a flat stencil brush and an up-and-down motion. A small foam roller is another great way to apply adhesive using stencils. Just be sure the glue is evenly distributed on the roller. The adhesives are easy to screen print and print beautifully through Thermofax screens. Handpainting is also an option. Size the scale of the lines or dots you want to make to the brush you choose.

Stamping prints the sheerest layer of glue on the fabric. The unique quality of the stamped image lies in its organic looseness, so choose stamping if you want texture or less-than-perfect images. Stenciling allows heavier glue application. Screen printing allows for the most consistent and even foil applications of all methods.

Adhesives should never be thinned with water, and never forget that the glue is always permanent when dry. If you don't like the images you have printed, you must wash them off immediately.

Directions

1 Fabric should be stabilized, clean, and dry. press wrinkled fabric.

2 Apply glue by stamping, stenciling, handpainting, or screen printing. Glue must be completely dry before the foil is applied. This can take an hour or more, based on how heavily the glue was applied.

3 You MUST work on a hard padded surface. An ironing board isn't usually strong enough to stand firm as you press. Use several layers of muslin on a counter top or table instead. Padding is needed, but the surface should not be soft.

4   Set your iron to high. Most irons don't get hot enough to work well at the medium setting; if you have an efficient iron, test whether it works best on medium or high.

5   A Teflon surface is invaluable to this process. If your iron does not have a Teflon coating, use a pressing cloth. This can absorb heat and make it harder to attain results, so experiment.

6   Work on small areas. It's harder to foil a big surface all at once. Work in sections. The cellophane layer is on the TOP. You are looking through it at the color. In order to keep this straight, use the foiling mantra: *see the color*. You must see the color to ensure the correct orientation of the foil sheet.

7   USE THE SIDE OR TIP OF THE IRON. The foil glue softens if you spend too much time heating it, and you run the risk of melting the foil. Push the side or tip of the iron very hard, scuffing over the foil surface. Push away from your body as you count 1, 2, 3. That should be long enough.

8   Peel the cellophane back. If the area isn't foiled completely, you can reapply. ■

Stenciled foil

Screen-printed foil

Screen-printed foil

Collaged
Fabric Panels

Mary Hettmansperger

WHETHER I'M WORKING ON JEWELRY, basketry, surface design, or quilting, I am enthralled with the process and details of connecting and piecing. Fiber basketry and jewelry are my main artistic focus. However, these quilted panels allow me to use many of the applications I find so appealing and explore new ways to apply my knowledge and creativity to the art of quilting that I love, including layering, weaving, and incorporating found objects and embellishments. Use these instructions to create a quilted panel of personal interpretation with found and assembled items.

Art by Mary Hettmansperger

materials

Batting or interfacing (to give the panels weight and density)	Thread for quilting and sewing
Decorative fat quarters in a variety of fabrics	18-gauge copper wire
Solid fabric for the panels	Beads for embellishment
Irish waxed linen (4- or 3-ply)	Washers
6" (15 cm) length of 26- or 24-gauge wire	Coins with holes
Size D Nymo beading thread	Flat disc beads
	A variety of found, recycled, and purchased items to attach

Directions

The finished project shown is a set of three panels all hung together, but you can choose to do one panel or any multiple to create a variety of looks.

1 Decide on the panel size you desire. Cut two pieces of fabric (the front and back) to the dimensions you've chosen. Cut the batting or interfacing the same size. (I use a variety of battings or interfacings, depending on the look and stiffness I am trying to achieve.)

2 Pin all three layers to hold the fabric in place, or baste if you prefer. Begin at one end of the quilt sandwich and quilt vertical lines. These lines can be evenly spaced, overlapped, or wavy.

3 Bind the piece with strips of the same fabric.

4 Cut decorative fat quarter fabrics into random-sized squares and rectangles. Sew the fabrics together using straight seams.

5 After you have sewn together a variety of fabrics in no particular order or measurement, cut the pieced fabric, then sew these pieces back together in a new arrangement. Make only squares, rectangles, and straight strips. Decide on the final shape of the collage fabric (e.g., series of squares, one long panel, etc.). When you have a successful collage of pieces sewn together and the shape decided, square up the decorative fabric to begin the surface design.

6 Arrange your found items on the fabric, leaving some of the spaces empty to show off the fabric. Attach the items to the squares by hand, using beading thread. Make stacks of flat items to give dimension. Attach small beads for added detail. Add some hand embroidery for more interest.

7 Once the surface embellishment is complete, fold the raw edge of the collaged fabric to the back side and place the embellished fabric on the panel. Sew the embellished pieces of fabric onto the panels with a buttonhole stitch. ■

Tips

• If your surface embellishments are not too large and will not get in the way of the sewing machine, you can always sew them on that way. I prefer handstitching them to the panel and adding further tacking stitches to make sure the elements are secure.

• Fabric for a hanger can be sewn to the top edge of the finished panel, or the finished hanger can be made by extending the decorative fabric, finishing the edge and turning it to the back side, and then securing it. Tabs can also be attached to the back side to create an invisible way to hang the panels.

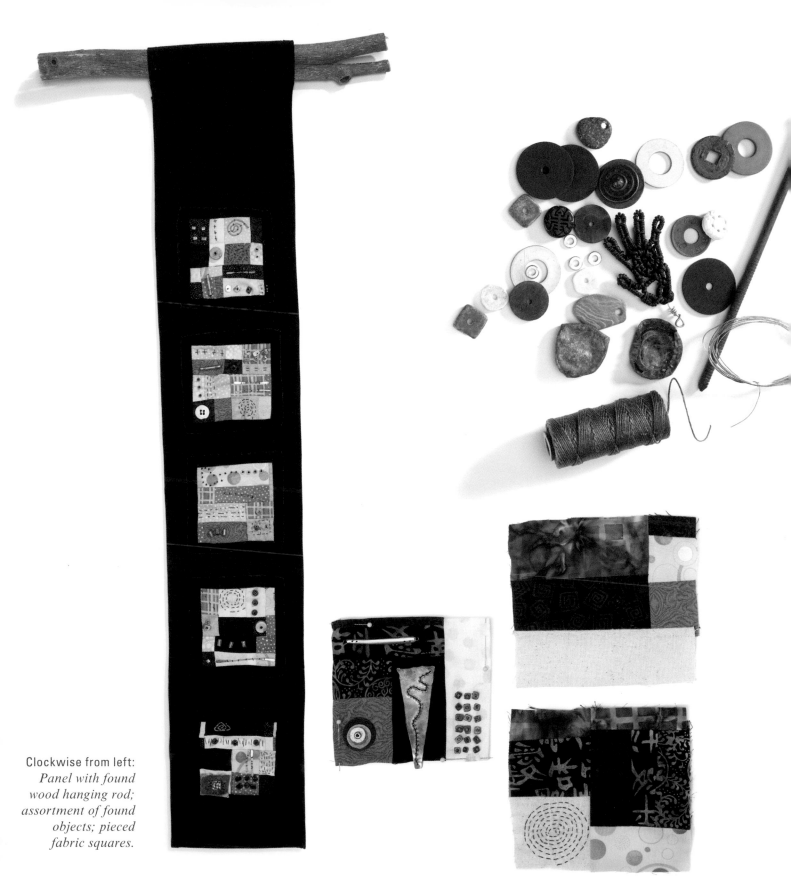

Clockwise from left:
*Panel with found
wood hanging rod;
assortment of found
objects; pieced
fabric squares.*

FlorAbundance

Embellished Patchwork Paper Collage

Jill A. Kennedy

*Art by
Jill A.
Kennedy*

FOR ME, NOTHING IS MORE SATISFYING than being able to create artwork that combines several of my favorite mixed-media art techniques with embroidery, incorporating, too, my passion for pattern and love of color.

materials

Construction paper or handmade paper a few sheets in different color tones

Wax crayons

Gold paint stick

Pointed tool such as an awl

Colored inks (or leftover fabric dyes)

Paintbrushes: soft bristle or sponge

½ yd (45.5 cm) fusible web with backing paper, such as WonderUnder

½ yd (45.5 cm) fusible interfacing

Parchment paper

Iron and ironing board

Sewing machine and accessories

Size 90 sewing machine needles

Machine threads: rayon, silk, polyneon, and metallic

Needles and hoop for hand embroidery

Scissors

Decorative yarns and threads

Felt

For embellishment:

Beads, sequins

Acrylic paints

Muslin

Rubber stamps and gold stamp pad

Soldering iron and heat-resistant mat

Sheer fabrics such as organza, twinkle, voile

Tissue paper or water-soluble stabilizer

Hoop for machine embroidery

Paper-fabric backgrounds

Make Background Paper

1 Choose a color scheme and gather your materials. Take three sheets of paper (construction or handmade) and draw shapes, patterns, and lines with colored wax crayons. Cover one sheet of paper with circular patterns, another with linear patterns, and the third sheet with just plain colored areas and no pattern. Push down firmly on the crayon to ensure that you leave enough wax on the paper's surface to resist the ink. Try rubbing the crayon sideways across the paper leaving a broken textured effect, as this will give nice resist results when the ink is brushed on top. Layer different colors on top of each other and leave some areas of the paper without crayon so that the ink will soak in, giving a contrast to the waxed areas. Build up a collection of at least three different decorated papers.

- -

Tip: Hard-wax crayons will resist the ink more than soft-wax crayons.

- -

2 Use a pointed tool to scratch into the wax to create marks and give texture. These marks will suggest areas to stitch later.

- -

Tip: For pattern inspiration, check out books on oriental rugs and carpets.

- -

3 Take a large soft paintbrush or a sponge brush and apply colored inks. Let them blend together and flood over the waxed paper, sponging off any excess if it gets too wet. Leave the papers to dry, allowing the ink to resist the wax.

4 To build up a rich surface, apply gold paint stick. Let the design guide you as to where to use it. Now apply a darker ink over the gold wax and leave the papers to dry again.

5 Iron the decorated papers between sheets of parchment paper, melting the wax into the

paper. Repeat with more wax crayon and ink. Dry the papers and iron once again.

Make Paper-Fabric

1 Iron a piece of iron-on interfacing to the backs of your papers. Use a medium heat, between the wool and cotton settings and remember to use parchment paper over and under your papers to protect them, as well as your iron and ironing surface.

- -

Tip: If you remove the backing paper while it is still warm, you will get a duller surface than if you leave the fusible to cool before removing the backing paper.

- -

2 Take a piece of fusible web and iron it to the fronts of the papers. Leave it to cool and then peel away the backing paper.

3 Now comes the really fun part! Taking your decorated papers in hand, completely crumple and scrunch them up. This will soften the fibers in the papers and make them feel more like fabric. Make sure you crumple them well all over, to ensure that sufficient softening occurs.

Assemble the Background

1 Lay out your papers and select areas from each to cut out; rearrange them to make one piece of paper-fabric. At this stage, do not worry about the finished size.

- -

Tip: Don't be afraid to cut the papers into halves, quarters, thirds, etc., mixing them together. Think about balancing the composition by choosing areas that have pattern and placing them next to areas without.

- -

2 When you have cut out the pieces, lay them face down in position on parchment paper. Make sure all of the edges butt up to each other, leaving no spaces or gaps between.

3 Lay a piece of iron-on interfacing on top, cover with more parchment paper, and iron well to fix it in place.

4 Determine your desired finished size and cut out your favorite area from the paper-fabric. I chose a 9" × 9" (23 × 23 cm) square.

Stitch and Embellish

Now that you have created your patchwork paper-fabric it is ready for embroidery, embellishment, and stitch.

FREE-MOTION EMBROIDERY

- -

Tip: You will not need to place the paper-fabric in a hoop as it is stiff enough to machine stitch without one.

- -

1 Set up your sewing machine for free-motion embroidery. Use a clear monofilament thread in the bobbin to save using your special threads. Use your thread of choice on the top. Select colors that match and complement your chosen color scheme.

- -

Tip: Be sure you use a large-eyed machine needle to cope with the metallic threads, the thickness of the paper-fabric, and the embellishments being stitched.

- -

2 Machine stitch along the lines forming the patterns; use both straight and varied-width zigzag stitches. Working from light to dark, change threads regularly, building up an interesting stitched surface. Variegated threads look good, too, and add subtle color changes. Do not over-stitch the paper-fabric; aim to enhance the design with stitching that still allows the design to show through.

3 To add a different stitched texture to the surface, wind embroidery floss onto the bobbin, bypassing the tension spring in your machine, and machine a straight stitch

upside down. Be sure to lower the upper tension before stitching. Draw a pattern onto the wrong side of the paper-fabric where you wish to place your design, and machine stitch following the drawn lines. Alternatively, for a more random effect, use a vermicelli stitch.

4 Choose some space-dyed knitted ribbon, or similar, and couch this into place using a free-motion stitch or any pattern stitch that's built into your sewing machine. Again, be guided by the design you drew on the paper for placement of the couched ribbon. Lightly zigzag around all four outside edges of the paper-fabric.

HANDSTITCHING

To add contrast to the free-motion stitching, incorporate a variety of hand-embroidery stitches, again picking out details in the design to help with placement. There are many books available on the market covering hand-embroidery stitches.

I have used a simple running stitch, backstitch, and French knots; be as adventurous as you like.

Look for spaces inside areas in the design that need accentuating. Use metallic yarn or embroidery floss and work long straight stitches across the space. Vary the thickness and type of fiber you use for added textural interest.

Work French knots in the centers of circles and swirls, etc. Grouping them together creates a raised, textured area.

- -

Tip: A running stitch or backstitch makes a good outline and/or border stitch. Using these on top of the machine stitching will add depth to the design.

- -

EMBELLISHMENTS

I love to create a variety of embellishments for my pieces. I make embroidered floral motifs primarily using two substrates: a painted and stamped muslin and layers of sheer fabrics. These motifs can be digitally embroidered or free-motion embroidered. I also create what I call cutwork ribbon, or a ribbon of stitched circles. And finally, I create my own cords for embellishing my work.

When you've created your embellishments, the fun is in deciding where to position them. Maintain a balanced composition and place the embellishments where they will make the most impact.

The floral motifs form the main focal point of the collage as they are large and stand proud on the decorated surface. Using a clear thread, stitch a few stitches around each flower center—just enough to hold them in place. You can layer a small motif on top of a large motif to create more depth.

Cut your cutwork ribbon to length, arrange it as you desire, and stitch it in place. I like to lay it half off one edge—this creates more interest and attracts the eye. Then I place another piece on the collage in a different direction, again having the end slightly overhang the edge.

Loop the cord down one edge, stitching it in place as you go. I left the tail long enough to couch down in a curlicue design on the surface of my piece.

Take another length of cord and tie knots every inch or so to add another feature to the edge of the collage; stitch this in place.

Introduce fine detail to the collage by sewing on beads and sequins to accentuate the couched lines, heighten the stitched areas, and, of course, add some sparkle.

Finishing

When all stitching is complete, cut a piece of felt to size and sew this to the wrong side of your patchwork paper collage to neaten the back. ■

Couched threads

Free-motion stitching

Free-motion stitching

*Art by Judy
Coates Perez*

Tea
and
Entomology

Judy Coates Perez

I LOVE EXPERIMENTING with unusual fibers in my quilting, so when I saw the True Colors challenge for paper quilts to be displayed at the Make It University! with *Cloth Paper Scissors* area at the International Quilt Festival in Chicago, I thought this would be a perfect opportunity to spread my creative wings. I love working on paper and fabric; combining the two seemed like the best of both worlds. As I was thinking about what to do for this challenge, my eyes were drawn to the dried tea bag sitting next to my daily cup, and my mind was awash with new possibilities.

materials

White cotton fabric, at least
14" × 14" (35.5 × 35.5 cm)

Tea bags

Permanent ink pen

Collage papers such as tea labels, dry
cleaning tags, and sewing patterns

Fabric printed using a
toner-based copier

Textile paints

Acrylic matte medium

Brayer

Rubber stamps

Tsukineko inks

Shiva Paintstiks

Colored pencils

Wool felt, 12" × 12" (30.5 × 30.5 cm)

Fusible web

Directions

1 Make some tea and then let a few of the used bags dry out. Carefully open the bags and pour out the dried leaves.

2 Draw a design onto the tea bag with a permanent ink pen. I already had a pen-and-ink drawing of a beetle in my sketchbook that was just the right size, so I laid my tea bag on top and traced over it. Because the tea bag paper is porous, the ink bleeds through to the surface underneath, so be sure to put a plain sheet of paper underneath. Repeat this step with more images.

3 Pull out your collection of collage scraps. Mine includes technical drawings and engravings that I have gathered from copyright-free sources, product labels (tea companies often have very nice ones), dry-cleaner tags, stamps, and old dress patterns from high school days. Choose a few pieces that appeal to you and set them aside.

4 Take a piece of white fabric and paint it with textile paint in the colors of your choice as a base. Let dry.

5 Next, adhere the tea bags to the painted fabric using acrylic matte medium. Brush the acrylic matte medium onto the painted surface, put down your tea bag paper (rolling a brayer over the paper helps to make a good bond), and then brush over the element with more acrylic matte medium to seal it. The interesting thing is that the paper from the tea bag will become almost invisible.

After collaging the rest of the tea bags to the fabric, I added tea labels, dry-cleaning tags, a torn piece of sewing-pattern tissue, and some printed fabric I had made several years ago by running it through a toner-based copy machine.

6 Add subtle color to the illustrations by painting sheer glazes over them with watered-down textile paint, slowly building up the intensity of color (I added text and pattern to the background with rubber stamps and Tsukineko ink).

7 When the piece is completely dry, cut the finished fabric to 14" × 14" (35.5 × 35.5 cm) and fuse it to the felt, centering the felt on the back of the painted fabric. (I chose wool felt over batting because I wanted a flat, smooth surface for this quilt.) Fold the edges of the painted fabric over to the back of the felt and fuse them in place. This makes a nice flat and flexible piece for stitching that does not require a binding.

8 Quilt the piece using the pattern of your choice. I decided to take a risk and use quilting that was totally unrelated to the design of the piece, yet was related to the aesthetic of the piece.

I found a gothic tile design in a book of historic ornament that I modified into a pattern to be quilted. I traced the design onto tracing paper with a fine-point marker and taped it to my quilt in two areas that had no stitching. Then I quilted the piece through the tracing paper, stitching on my drawn lines. After all the stitching was done, I carefully tore the tracing paper away.

9 When you are finished quilting, you may want to give the shapes more depth by creating visual layers. I shaded portions of the stitched pattern with a copper-colored Shiva Paintstik. When I stood back and looked at the piece, the bird and butterfly started to feel lost in the design, so I added a little color to them with some colored pencils and lightened up some of the areas around them with a cream-colored pencil. The paper on top of the fabric allowed the colored pencils to go on creamy and smooth.

So, when the day was over my little tea bag made not only a good cuppa tea, but a satisfying finished piece of art. ■

Apply tea bag and collage papers to the painted fabric with acrylic matte medium.

When your collage has dried, cut it to 14" × 14" (35.5 × 35.5 cm). Fuse wool felt to the back of the collaged fabric, folding the extra inch all around to the back of the felt.

preparing a tea bag for art

1   After steeping your tea, set the tea bag on the counter to dry and enjoy that fabulous warm cuppa tea with a dash of cream.

2   When the tea bag is completely dry (not damp) carefully remove the staple, unfold the top of the bag, and shake out the dried tea leaves into the trash, unless you have thought of some way to incorporate these into your art. So far it has not occurred to me, but give me time . . .

3   Gently pull the seam apart down the length of the bag and fold it out flat, brushing away any leaves that may be clinging to the paper.

I traced a design onto tracing paper, overlaid it onto the fabric, and stitched over the lines to quilt the piece.

BRANDING FOR ARTISTS

Jane Dávila

ARTISTS CAN ADAPT some of the methods that the corporate world uses to sell their art. Branding is a prime example of one of these methods and is an extremely effective tool for increasing sales. Companies and celebrities work hard to stand out from one another and create a unique impression; artists can benefit from doing the same.

Your brand should go beyond a clever slogan or beautiful logo to create a lasting impression on the consumer, building loyalty and recognition.

While branding may seem like a very commercial way of viewing yourself, it is an indispensable tool if your goal is to sell more art. Your brand represents a partnership between your art and your identity. It should present you to the world in a clear, concise, and unique manner so that your work is immediately identifiable.

Define Your Brand

You can start to define your brand by asking yourself a few simple questions about your work, broken into three categories: style, process, and content.

WHAT IS YOUR STYLE? Is your work whimsical, political, sophisticated, or rustic?

WHAT IS YOUR PROCESS? Is your work created with the latest digital technology and state-of-the-art materials, or is it laboriously handcrafted using traditional techniques? What is unique about your method of working? Do you use an unusual technique, or did you develop and adapt a process from another medium?

WHAT CONTENT DOES YOUR WORK DEPICT? Is your work abstract, do you create landscapes, or do you reference a specific culture or period in time? Do you have a signature motif or image that often appears in your work?

Ask yourself about the relationship between your personality and your artistic expression. Are they similar or quite different? What is the core message of your work? What is your passion and how does it show in your work? Is there something unique and memorable about you or your life? What do you want others to think of when they think of you and your work? Can you define your personality in a short phrase that describes you and no one else?

Be as specific as possible, but keep it simple. Ask a few trusted friends and colleagues some of these questions for additional input. Put a lot of thought into developing your brand; you don't want to change your mind after a short time. Take your time and get it right.

So, now that you've determined that you are a third-generation Southern art quilter specializing in quirky pop-art pet portraiture using hand-dyed and recycled materials, you can make some decisions about how to create your brand and present it to the world.

Create Your Brand

Using the answers to the aforementioned questions, create a signature look for your brand that you can transmit at every point of contact with your public. Based on your newly defined brand, choose a color story to use in all print and online media. If you are the Crazy Quilting Cowgirl, select colors that will help people relate to that brand. Use these colors

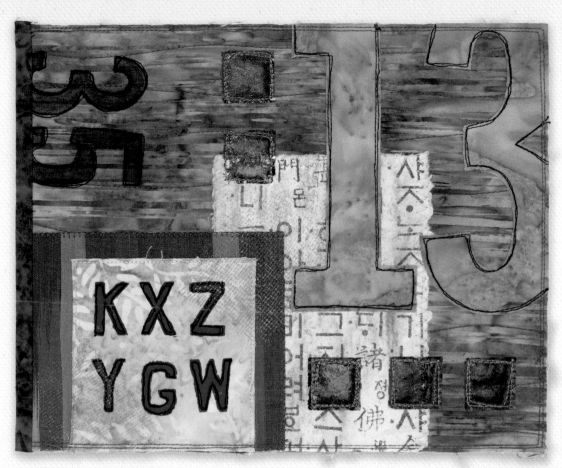

Safety in Numbers
8" × 10"
(20.5 × 25.5 cm)

consistently in your business cards, in other printed material, and on your website and blog.

Choose a logo based on your work and identity as an artist. Fortunately, as visual artists, we have a wealth of imagery within our own art from which to draw.

Promote Your Brand

The key to promoting your brand is to be consistent and persistent. Once your logo and color story are determined, use them to build recognition. Keep your brand in mind for all decisions related to how you present yourself and your art. Repeated use will raise awareness of you and your work, but a scattered and inconsistent approach will lead to confusion.

If you have a slogan or a short phrase to describe your brand, use it everywhere so it becomes associated with you and your work. You want it to stick in your customers' minds

and create an indelible impression. Place your slogan at the bottom of every email. Add it to your profile on social networking sites and to your email newsletters. Repetition is the most effective way to build your brand.

Be authentic when establishing your brand. Don't try to be something you are not; it will show, and people will remember you for the wrong reasons. Use your real name on social media sites. Use a photo that reflects your brand as an avatar on Twitter, Facebook, and in the quiltingarts.com forums. This will most likely be a photo of you, but it could also be your logo or a photo of your work.

Remember that the purpose of your brand is to help you attract, connect with, and retain customers. It helps define who you are and what you stand for; it should set you apart from other artists and infuse your work with a unique and memorable identity. ■

About the Contributors

FRANCES HOLLIDAY ALFORD found her way into quilting arts after many journeys into other disciplines. Her pieces are often painted, stitched, or drawn to reflect her vision and painterly aesthetic. Frances also enjoys making heavily embellished pieces, claiming that if she can sew it down, she will use it. Her pieces always have a narrative undertone, whether humorous or subtle. Frances lives in Grafton, Vermont, with a studio near her historic home. A retired special education teacher, art quilting is now her professional focus. *franceshollidayalford.com*

FRIEDA ANDERSON made her first quilt in high school and has been designing and making original quilts ever since. Most of her quilts are fused or have fusing in them; her work is machine-quilted and nature-inspired. She discovered the process of hand-dyeing fabric twenty years ago and today works almost exclusively with her own hand-dyed cottons and silks. Frieda also has her own line of fused wall-quilt patterns. *friestyle.com*

ANA BUZZALINO is a quiltmaker, fiber artist, and teacher living in Calgary, Alberta, Canada. Ana's work has been featured in *Quilting Arts* Calendar and *Quilting Arts* magazine, and she has appeared on *Quilting Arts TV* Series 800. Her work has been juried into national and international shows. Ana's newest work incorporates paint and stitch to add texture to the quilted surface. *patchesandpaint.com*

SUE CAVANAUGH is an expert in the ancient art of stitch-resist shibori. Her work has appeared in exhibits including Quilt National and Visions and in publications including *The Art Quilt Collection* (Sixth and Spring, 2010), *1000 Artisan Textiles* (Quarry, 2010), and *Surface Design Newsletter*. Sue received the Lynn Goodwin Borgman Award for Surface Design at Quilt National 2009 and Best of Show at the 2008 Shibori Cut Loose exhibition in Minneapolis. Circle Galleries

in Columbus, Ohio, and gráficas gallery in Nantucket, Massachusetts, represent Sue. Her studio is in her home in the Short North Arts District, Columbus, Ohio. *suecavanaughart.com*

JANE DÁVILA, a fiber and mixed-media artist, began her professional art career as a printmaker. Her work has been exhibitied in commercial galleries and placed in private and corporate collections worldwide. In the 1990s, she began working in fiber, quilting, and mixed media while still incorporating printmaking techniques. Jane is the author of *Jane Dávila's Surface Design Essentials* (C&T, 2010) and co-author with Elin Waterston of *Art Quilt Workbook* (C&T, 2007) and *Art Quilts at Play* (C&T, 2009). She is the editor of the eMag *Quilting Arts In Stitches*. Jane lives in Connecticut with her husband, Carlos, a painter and sculptor. *janedavila.com*

JANE DUNNEWOLD is the author of *Art Cloth* (Interweave, 2010), *Complex Cloth* (Martingale, 2000), and *Improvisational Screen Printing* (ArtCloth Studios, 2003), and the coauthor of *Finding Your Own Visual Language* (Committed to Cloth, 2007). Dunnewold teaches and lectures on mixed media and textiles internationally. She was awarded the Quilt Japan Prize in the 2002 Visions exhibition and received the Gold Prize at the Taegue International Textile Exhibition in Korea. *complexcloth.com*
existentialneighborhood.blogspot.com.

KAREN FRICKE is a quilt and fiber artist based in Rockville, Maryland. Karen began sewing in her grandmother's attic sewing room; both Karen and her grandmother became interested in quilting during the folk art revival of the 1970s. In recent years, she has focused her creative spirit into her quilts as a full-time artist. Much of her work is Judaic synagogue and ritual fiber art, which lends itself beautifully to quilting. *karenfrickequilts.com*

TERRY GRANT lives just outside Portland, Oregon, with her husband, Ray. She earned a degree in art and concentrated her energy on painting and printmaking. It wasn't until she saw a group of beautiful quilts that she knew her love of art and of textiles and sewing could be combined. Her work has been exhibited nationally and internationally and has appeared in a number of books. She is an author of *Twelve by Twelve: The International Art Quilt Challenge* (Lark, 2011). *andsewitgoes.blogspot.com*

MARY HETTMANSPERGER is a fiber and jewelry artist who teaches in the United States and internationally. Mary has authored and illustrated three books: *Fabulous Woven Jewelry* (Lark, 2006); *Wrap, Stitch, Fold & Rivet* (Lark, 2008); and *Mixed Metal Jewelry Workshop* (Lark, 2010). The Katie Gingrass Gallery has exhibited Mary's work at the International Sculpture Objects and Functional Art (SOFA) show. Mary has been a featured artist on PBS television shows *Beads, Baubles, and Jewels* and *Quilting Art,* and her work has appeared in *Quilting Arts, Art Jewelry, Bead & Button, Beadwork*, and other magazines. *maryhetts.com*

MELODY JOHNSON has been a quilt artist since 1981. Previously a professional dyer, she founded Artfabr!k with Laura Wasilowski. Melody has a degree in painting and drawing from Northeastern Illinois University and a master's degree in fibers from Northern Illinois University. Her award-winning quilts have been exhibited nationally and internationally, including three appearances in Quilt National. Melody is now retired in Tennessee, where she and her husband are learning to slow down and enjoy the moment. *fibermania.blogspot.com*

JILL A. KENNEDY is a passionate textile artist, embroiderer, and tutor who loves to work in mixed media. Her work combines bright colors with rich textures and patterns, using free machine and digital embroidery on unusual painted and distressed surfaces. Jill runs creative textile workshops in her hometown of Devon, England, and offers online tutorials through her website. She has written numerous articles for textile magazines and is a member of the Embroiderers' Guild. *craftsontheweb.co.uk*

LYNN KRAWCZYK is a mixed-media artist focusing on Thermofax screen printing and assemblages. Her work has appeared in several publications, including *Quilting Arts*, *Cloth Paper Scissors,* and *Sew Somerset* magazines, as well as numerous books. Her DVD, *Print Design Compose* (Interweave), teaches viewers to print fabrics and use them to design abstract art quilts. She lives in Plymouth, Michigan, with her West Highland terrier. *fibraartysta.blogspot.com*

ANNE LULLIE combines vibrant hand-dyed fabric, sensuous curved shapes, and fusible appliqué technique. Anne has exhibited her art quilts internationally, winning Second Place, Art Abstract, in Road to California 2010 and Best Machine Workmanship at American Quilter's Society Quilt Expo Des Moines 2008. Anne's quilts have appeared in *500 Art Quilts* (Lark, 2010), *Portfolio 16* and *Portfolio 17* (Studio Art Quilt Association), and other books and magazines. In 2005, Anne's *Colorplay I* traveled with the Husqvarna Viking exhibition Art Takes Shape and is now in the collection of Quilts Inc. *annelullie.com*

BONNIE MCCAFFERY teaches in countries around the world, including New Zealand, England, Ireland, Scotland, France, Sweden,

Denmark, Canada, Curacao, and Australia. She is the author of *Fantasy Fabrics* (Martingale, 1999), *Fantasy Floral Quilts* (Martingale, 2001), and *Portrait Quilts* (Dream Mountain Studios, 2005). Bonnie specializes in a technique she calls DoodleZenDotZ, combining doodles, bobbin embroidery, and dots of paint. She's also known for her free VidCasts, featuring demonstrations, quilt shows, and interviews with quilt personalities. *bonniemccaffery.com*

HEIDI MIRACLE-MCMAHILL is a fiber artist with a passion for color, texture, rhythm, and pattern. Professionally trained in the pastry arts, Heidi is a painter, quilter, stitcher, and beader. Her work is characterized by its sense of fun and spontaneity, and she is always experimenting with new techniques. Heidi especially enjoys working with water-soluble crayons on paper and fabric and carving blocks to create stamped images. Her quilts have been widely exhibited, and her Stitch Frenzy piece won Juror's First Choice Award at the 2007 National Small Art Quilts exhibition. *miracle-mcmahill.com*

JUDY COATES PEREZ is an award-winning textile artist known for her highly detailed, colorfully painted whole-cloth quilts. She earned a BFA from Otis/Parsons School of Design in Los Angeles, California, and teaches internationally. Exploring themes drawn from folklore, history, and nature, and blending quilting skills with techniques drawn from her graphic arts background, she uses textile paints, dyes, inks, acrylic powders, and artist's pencils on fabric. Judy has written numerous articles for *Quilting Arts* and *Cloth Paper Scissors* magazines, has been a frequent guest on *Quilting Arts TV,* and has made three instructional DVDs produced by Interweave. *judyperez.blogspot.com* *paintedthreadsprojects.blogspot.com*

DAREN PITTS REDMAN lives in Brown County, Indiana, where she experiences the four seasons in vibrant color. She dyes her own cotton and silk fabrics with fiber-reactive dyes and natural indigo dye, influenced by the palette of the trees and flowers that surround her. Daren uses *arashi* and *itajime* shibori techniques to create patterns on her fabrics and discovered art quilting after taking Nancy Crow's workshops in 2005. An avid international traveler, she photographs architecture, flowers, and patterns in tiles as inspiration for art. *web.me.com/darenpittsredman*

CONNIE ROSE is a surface designer and studio quilter living in rural Humboldt County, California. She has worked with textiles since the early 1970s, and her fiber arts background includes knitting, crocheting, spinning, weaving, and dyeing. Connie's inspirations include the natural world, Art Deco, ancient Egyptian and Native American designs, and ethnic tribal patterns. She teaches shibori dyeing, discharging, and other surface design workshops. *constancerosedesigns.blogspot.com*

SARAH ANN SMITH is spurred to create by color, line, texture, imagery, stories, and being part of the tradition of quilting and the future of quilting and art. She is a former U.S. diplomat with tours in Africa, South America, and North America; these, along with travels to Asia and Europe, influence her work. Sarah specializes in machine stitching and is the author of *Threadwork Unraveled* (American Quilter's Society, 2009). She lives in Hope, Maine. *sarahannsmith.com*

BELINDA SPIWAK is an elementary school teacher and mixed-media artist who creates art quilts and art journals. Her work has appeared in *Cloth Paper Scissors, Quilting Arts, International Quilt Festival Quilt Scene*, and *Cloth Paper Scissors*

Studios magazines, as well as the book *Stitch Alchemy* by Kelli Perkins (Interweave, 2009). Belinda teaches mixed-media art in the Chicago area and owns the Mixed Media Art Friends Yahoo group. *alteredbelly.blogspot.com*

BERYL TAYLOR was born in Rotherham, England, and attended the Manchester High School of Art. She completed the City and Guilds Creative Embroidery program and started the textile group Threadmill with other City and Guilds graduates. Beryl works as a mixed-media artist in Monroe Township, New Jersey. She dyes, paints, stamps, embroiders, and decorates papers, and other media to produce textured effects and vibrant colors. She is the author of *Mixed Media Explorations* (Quilting Arts, 2006) and has made several appearances on *Quilting Arts TV*. *beryltaylor.com*

MELANIE TESTA inspires with imaginative work. She paints and dyes cotton, silk organza, threads, and bindings, and she also finds time to journal, paint on stretched canvas, and make mixed-media art. Melanie thrives in hopping and artistic Brooklyn, New York. She is the author of *Inspired to Quilt: Creative Experiments in Art Quilt Imagery* (Interweave, 2009) and has a workshop on DVD titled *Print, Collage, Quilt*. *melanietesta.com*

LAURA WASILOWSKI creates art quilts in her home studio in Elgin, Illinois. Her colorful and whimsical quilts have been exhibited internationally and can be found in corporate, museum, and private collections. With a background in fabric dyeing and costume design, Laura travels the world as a quilt instructor, lecturer, and author of *Fanciful Stitches, Colorful Quilts* (C&T, 2011). Inspired by nature, everyday objects, and stores about family, friends, and home, Laura creates artwork in an improvisational manner by fusing fabrics and applying machine and handstitching. *artfabrik.com*

CAROL WATKINS is a textile artist whose work combines photographic imagery on fabric in art quilts and densely stitched, highly detailed thread paintings. Her art has been juried into many exhibitions including Quilt National 2011, published in magazines and books including *500 Art Quilts* (Lark, 2010), and is a part of many private and public collections. Carol has been an artist in residence at Rocky Mountain National Park and at Mesa Verde National Park; her passion for nature and for exploring the world around her provides the impetus for her fiber art. *carolwatkins.com*

ENID GJELTEN WEICHSELBAUM began to make art as a child. She studied art and languages in Iowa and in Norway where she developed a keen interest in Viking art and Scandinavian design. Enid went on to teach languages, followed by a career in marketing that took her around the world—but always with an art project in hand. As an art quilter, Enid loves all kinds of textures and fibers and interpreting experiences and favorite images into wall quilts. *enidgjelten.com*

LENI LEVENSON WIENER is an art quilter, author, and instructor living outside New York City. She describes her work, which has been exhibited in the United States and abroad, as fabric collage with thread-painted details. A former commercial photographer, Leni is drawn to subjects that are photographic in nature. All of her pieces begin with a photograph or combination of photographs that are translated into commercially available fabric. Leni is the author of *Thread Painting* (Krause, 2007), *Photo-Inspired Art Quilts* (Krause, 2009), and *3-Fabric Quilts* (Krause, 2011). *leniwiener.com*

Resources

SUPPLIERS

Dharma Trading Co.
dharmatrading.com
(800) 542-5227
PFD fabrics and blanks, textile paints
and dyes, surface design supplies.

Dick Blick Art Materials
dickblick.com
(800) 828-4548
Full range of art and surface design supplies.

eQuilter.com
equilter.com
(877) 322-7423
More than 22,000 fabrics in stock;
batting, threads, notions.

InterweaveStore
interweavestore.com
Books, magazines, DVDs, supplies
for art quilting and mixed media.

MeinkeToy
meinketoy.com
(248) 813-9806
Full range of fiber art supplies.

PRO Chemical & Dye
prochemicalanddye.com
(800) 228-9393
Dyes and dyeing supplies,
textile paints, and more.

The Thread Studio (Australia)
thethreadstudio.com
Extensive range of threads, fibers,
and embellishments.

ADDITIONAL READING

There are many wonderful books on art-
quilting techniques and inspiration;
here are just a few of our favorites.

Bolton, Patricia. *The Quilting Arts Book:
Techniques and Inspiration for Creating One-
of-a-Kind Quilts.* Interweave, 2008.

Brackmann, Holly. *The Surface Designer's
Handbook: Dyeing, Printing, Painting, and
Creating Resists on Fabric.* Interweave, 2006.

Dávila, Jane, and Elin Waterston. *Art
Quilt Workbook: Exercises & Techniques
to Ignite Your Creativity.* C&T, 2007.

Dunnewold, Jane. *Art Cloth: A Guide to
Surface Design for Fabric.* Interweave, 2010.

Dunnewold, Jane. *Complex Cloth.* Martingale, 1996.

Kemshall, Linda, and Laura Kemshall. *The
Painted Quilt: Paint and Print Techniques
for Color on Quilts.* F&W, 2007.

Kinard, Lyric. *Art + Quilt: Design Principles
and Creativity Exercises.* Interweave, 2009.

Meech, Sandra. *Creative Quilts: Inspiration,
Texture & Stitch.* Batsford, 2006.

Testa, Melanie. *Inspired to Quilt: Creative
Experiments in Art Quilt Imagery.* Interweave, 2009.

Wells, Jean. *Intuitive Color & Design:
Adventures in Art Quilting.* C&T, 2009.

Williamson, Jeanne. *The Uncommon Quilter:
Small Art Quilts Created with Paper, Plastic,
Fiber, and Surface Design.* Potter Craft, 2007.

Index

Enjoy more **creative quilting ideas and solutions** with these innovative resources from *Interweave*

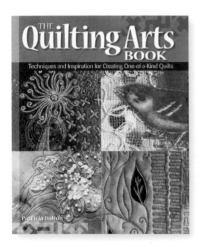

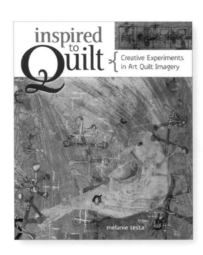

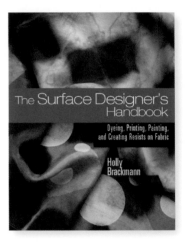

THE QUILTING ARTS BOOK
Techniques and Inspiration for Creating One-of-a-Kind Quilts

Patricia Bolton

ISBN 978-1-59668-099-9

$24.95

INSPIRED TO QUILT
Creative Experiments in Art Quilt Imagery

Melanie Testa

ISBN 978-1-59668-096-8

$24.95

THE SURFACE DESIGNER'S HANDBOOK
Dyeing, Printing, Painting, and Creating Resists on Fabric

Holly Brackmann

ISBN 978-1-931499-90-3

$29.95

Whether you consider yourself a contemporary quilter, fiber artist, art quilter, or wearable art artist, *Quilting Arts* magazine strives to meet your creative needs.
Quiltingdaily.com

Quilting Daily

Quiltingdaily.com, the online contemporary quilting community, offers free patterns, expert tips and techniques, e-newsletters, blogs, forums, videos, special offers, and more!
Quiltingdaily.com

Quilting Daily Shop
shop.quiltingdaily.com